Golfing
Gems

THE CONNOISSEURS GUIDE
TO GOLF COURSES IN

IRELAND

First published in Great Britain 1997 by
BEACON BOOKS
Barn Oast, Woodfalls Industrial Estate, Laddingford, Maidstone, Kent ME18 6DA.

ISBN 1 901839 02 8

© Finley Brand Communications Ltd. 1997

The moral right of the publisher has been asserted.

Distributed by Macmillan Distribution Ltd. 01256 29242

Cover Design by Roland Davies.

Course descriptions written by Alistair Tait.

Photography by Allsport and Mark Newcombe,
with additional photographs from Matthew Harris and Golf in Ireland.

Typesetting by Typecast, East Peckham.

Repro by Chameleon Colour, Tonbridge.

Printed and bound in Italy.

This book may be ordered by post direct from the publisher, but please try your book shop first.
Corporate editions and personal subscriptions of any of the Beacon Book guides are available.
Call for details – tel: 01622 872400.

Also published in the series: **Golfing Gems of England & Wales**
                               Golfing Gems of Scotland

Golf Monthly is published on the first Thursday of every month by IPC Magazines
Limited, King's Reach Tower, Stamford Street, London SE1 9LS. For subscription
enquiries call: 01444 445555 (fax no: 01444 445599) or write to: Quadrant Subscription
Services, FREEPOST CY1061, Haywards Heath, West Sussex RH16 3ZA.

Contents

Acknowledgements

As with any new book there have been many people who have contributed enormously and without whose help the 'Gems' would have remained hidden. We thank them all but in particular wish to express our sincerest appreciation to the following: To Christine for keeping us organised, to Mike for his stylish subbing, to Nicola for keeping our spirits up and to Daisy for keeping us on our toes. But finally to you dear reader for deeming our effort worthy of your hard-earned cash. Many thanks.

Andrew Finley   *Robert Brand*

Foreword

Ireland

*T*here is a school of thought which insists that a golfer has to travel to Scotland to have the chance to play on the world's finest links courses and, I suppose, it is correct up to a point.

Scotland is blessed with a series of sensational seaside courses, but it doesn't have a monopoly on them, as some people seem to think.

At the risk of being accused of being unpatriotic about my homeland, I would have to admit that Ireland has just as impressive a reservoir of great links courses, and inland courses too, although, for the most part, the Irish courses tend not to have such a high profile as their Scottish counterparts.

I am a committed Irophile – although I don't suppose for a second that's an actual word – and I take no persuasion whatsoever to travel to Ireland for a bit of light relaxation on the links. I admit I'm also a huge fan of the native Guinness and the combination of the two is something which I have never been able to resist.

As far as I'm concerned, and I know I'm not alone in this, Ireland comes right at the top of my list of favourite golfing destinations. Both north and south of the border, it has something for every travelling golfer, and the only problem is knowing where to start.

Over the years I've made dozens of pilgrimages to Ireland and during that time I don't think I've ever had a major disappointment. There are some courses which I've liked more than others – Royal County Down, Royal Portrush and Lahinch for example – but I don't think I've ever played a bad one. Ireland is crammed full of great courses, big and small. A bit like in Scotland, each small town seems to have one, and most welcome visitors with open arms.

This *Golf Monthly Connoisseurs Guide To Golf Courses In Ireland* doesn't pretend to be encyclopaedic. Like the compendiums of courses in Scotland and England & Wales, it was never meant to be, but in it we have selected 60 of what we consider to be the best of Ireland's most attractive courses, and we commend it for you for that reason. *Golf Monthly's Golfing Gems in Ireland* gives you a flavour of what Irish golf is all about, but what it can't do is to paint the whole picture. Golf in Ireland is an experience like no other. I suggest you try it, and see what I mean. You won't be disappointed.

Colin Callander

Regional Introduction Photographs:

Northern Ireland - *Royal County Down*

North West- *Ballyliffin*

South West - *Waterville*

South East - *Mount Juliet*

Dublin - *Druids Glen*

North East - *The Island Club*

Back Cover - *Ballyliffin*

Introduction

*W*elcome to *Golf Monthly Golfing Gems of Ireland,* the guide book written by golfers for golfers. Our aim has been to produce a series of guides for the touring golfer which will give not just the basic facts and geography of a course but will convey some sense of the atmosphere, the environment, the whole 'feel' that makes a great golf course what it is and often makes a less-than-famous course well worth a detour from the golfing equivalent of a motorway map.

Not that our 'Gems' are always hidden – it's just that some may be unfamiliar. But that is their attraction. One thing characterises them all – they have been chosen and described by *Golf Monthly* writers who have themselves enjoyed playing them. The clubs have not paid for their entries so what you have is a selection of courses guided only by the writers' belief that these are the courses the visitor will find rewarding and hospitable.

Here, then, are descriptions of 60 Irish courses you will be delighted to play. They all offer an intriguing – sometimes robust – challenge to your golfing ability and, unfailingly, a warm welcome and glorious scenery.

Keep the guide in your car, it will become an essential companion when travelling on business or pleasure. The hotels featured have, in nearly all cases, been recommended by the relevant golf club and we feel sure that you will find them an excellent place to stay, be it for one night or a long weekend. Often the proprietors are keen golfers themselves ensuring good local knowledge and a steady supply of sympathy!

Other books in this series cover England & Wales and Scotland with more planned for the near future. Each year the listings will be reviewed to ensure that quality is maintained. To help us in this task, should you have any comments please contact us at *Golf Monthly,* we will be pleased to hear from you.

Happy golfing!

* Whether indicated or not in the guide it will always be advisable to book your tee-time in advance and establish questions of dress code etc. to avoid possible embarrassment.

**In the Republic of Ireland some clubs express their card of the course in metres; in the editorial text, for the sake of continuity, yardage is used.

International Dialling Codes

From UK to Eire	00353	(delete first 0 of local number)
From Eire to NI	0044	(delete first 0 of local number)
From USA	011353	(delete first 0 of local number)

Northern Ireland

Northern Ireland

Read any list of top 100 courses in the British Isles, and you will find two of Northern Ireland's courses well up the rankings. Indeed, play Royal County Down and Royal Portrush and they will shoot to the top of your personal list of best courses. Portrush and County down are two courses worthy of their Royal status, for they are man-sized golf courses, championship layouts in every sense of the word. This is links golf at its best, with everything you expect to find on seaside courses - blind shots, deep pot bunkers, fast running fairways, undulating greens and strong winds. Not golf for the fainthearted, to be sure. These two magnificent layouts have been on the itinerary of nearly every visiting golfer down through the years, and they can get quite busy during the summer months. Don't despair, though, for there are plenty of great courses throughout the region to keep every level of golfer happy. Even if you weren't intent on playing golf, you would be attracted to the coastline north of Belfast. The stretch of shoreline along the Antrim Coast is simply spectacular. It's along this coastline that you will find the Giant's Causeway, a fascinating geological formation that appears to be steps either leading into or coming from the sea. Legend has it that the Irish Giant Finn McCool built these steps to help him make his way to the Scottish isle of Staffa to woo a female giant on that island. The Giant's Causeway is just a few miles away from Royal Portrush and is a must sight to visit while in the area. Make sure you take the walk down to see the rock formations close up. Although there is a very good visitor centre which tells the whole story, there is no substitute for getting up close because the Causeway has to be seen to believed. Something else that has to be seen to believed is the links course at Portstewart. To stand on the first tee is to experience one of the best views in all of golf. Portstewart has benefited from new holes created in the dunes which transformed the original course from a good links to a great one. Portstewart and Portrush are just two of four good links on this stretch of the

Antrim Coast. The other two are Castlerock and Ballycastle. These four layouts are used for the annual Black Bush Causeway Coast Tournament, a 72-hole stableford event sponsored by Bushmills Distillery, makers of Black Bush. And if you can squeeze in a visit to the Distillery in the little town by the same name, then your trip will be complete. The Antrim Coast and its fabulous courses are only an hour's drive away from the city of Belfast and good parkland courses such as Malone, Belvoir Park, Royal Belfast and Malone. Not much further south you will find Clandeboye and its two good courses. In fact, you could enjoy a round at a fine course in and around Belfast, enjoy a leisurely lunch and an equally leisurely drive and, in the height of summer at least, still be back on the Antrim coast for another round before a late tea. What more could you want for in life?

ROYAL COUNTY DOWN
ARDGLASS
MALONE
CLANDEBOYE
BELVOIR PARK

BALLYCASTLE
CASTLEROCK
ROYAL PORTRUSH
PORTSTEWART

Royal County Down

Consult any list of top golf courses in any magazine around the world, and you will find Royal County Down not far from the top. Play one round and you'll know why.

Old Tom Morris is the man originally responsible for Royal County Down. He laid out the course in 1889. Although many changes have been made to the layout over the years, it is definitely old style traditional golf, stuff Old Tom would be proud of.

You will find quite a few white rocks at County Down. You'll notice them from the tees. What you won't notice are fairways. The white rocks are your line to the fairway, for there are many blind tee shots on this fabulous links. Thankfully that's not the case for the approaches to the greens.

County Down is everything links golf should be – undulating greens, deep pot bunkers and tight fairway lies. Then there's the wind, always

the wind. The key to playing the course successfully lies in keeping the ball in play. Stray from the fairways and you'll have a job not only making par, but finding your ball, for the rough at County Down takes no prisoners.

The setting also makes Royal County Down one of the most beautiful courses in the world – it would certainly make an artist drool. In the background always are the Mourne Mountains, rising majestically to provide a backdrop for many approach shots. Play it in spring when the gorse is in bloom and you will experience one of the most pleasant walks in golf.

For years Royal County Down was virtually ignored by foreign visitors, but the word has been spread far and wide and now it's on everyone's must play list. In other words, don't expect to just show up and get a game. It pays to write well in advance – it's also well worth the effort.

COURSE INFORMATION & FACILITIES

Royal County Down
36 Golf Links Road, Newcastle,
Co. Down.

Secretary: Peter Rolph.
Tel: 013967-23314. Fax: 013967-26281.

Golf Professional Tel: 013967-22419.

Green Fees:
Weekdays – £60. Weekends – £70.
Weekdays (day) – £90. Weekends (day) – £100.

CARD OF THE COURSE – PAR 71

1	2	3	4	5	6	7	8	9	Out
506	424	473	217	440	396	145	428	486	3515
Par 5	Par 4	Par 4	Par 3	Par 4	Par 4	Par 3	Par 4	Par 4	Par 35

10	11	12	13	14	15	16	17	18	In
200	440	501	445	213	445	265	400	545	3454
Par 3	Par 4	Par 5	Par 4	Par 3	Par 4	Par 4	Par 4	Par 5	Par 36

HOW TO GET THERE

Newcastle is 30 miles south of Belfast via the A24; 90 miles north of Dublin via the N1 to Newry, and 25 miles east of Newry via the A25.

Ardglass

*T*he lovely links course of Ardglass lies not too far from Royal County Down, and while it may not be the test that Down is, it's a lot of fun.

Like it's Royal counterpart, Ardglass is a links, offers good views of the Irish Sea and the Mourne Mountains, and has some testing holes. Indeed, you're presented with a test almost right away, when you step onto the second tee. This is a par-3 of just 173-yards, but the danger here is the Irish Sea. Hit short or left and you'll be looking for your swimming trunks to play your next shot.

The second is just one of six par-3s on the Ardglass layout. Four of these one shotters call for fairly easy short iron or wedge approach shots. The 9th hole doesn't. At 205-yards; it calls for a full blooded 3-wood or 2-iron, depending on how far you hit the ball.

Ardglass is fairly short, just nudging over the 6,000 yard mark, but don't let that fool you. The wind often blows here, as it does at County Down, making a mockery of the yardage indicated on the card.

Like many Irish courses, there are remnants of a bygone age in evidence at Ardglass. Beside the clubhouse lie the remains of a Norman Castle built in 1177. The course hasn't quite been around that long, but it dates to 1896 when nine holes were constructed beside the sea. Nine more holes were added in 1971 to make it a proper course.

On a good day you can see the Isle of Man clearly; if you can't then you may be in for a tough round.

proximately 7 miles from
wnpatrick on B1.

Ardglass
Golf Club

COURSE INFORMATION & FACILITIES

 Ardglass Golf Club
Castle Place, Ardglass,
Co. Down.

Secretary: Miss Debbie Polly.
Tel: 01396-841219. Fax: 01396-841841.

Golf Professional Tel: 01396-841022.

Green Fees:
Weekdays – £14. Weekends – £20.
Weekdays (day) – £14. Weekends (day) – £20.

CARD OF THE COURSE – PAR 70

1	2	3	4	5	6	7	8	9	Out
292	173	269	351	135	485	507	394	205	2811
Par 4	Par 3	Par 4	Par 4	Par 3	Par 5	Par 5	Par 4	Par 3	Par 35

10	11	12	13	14	15	16	17	18	In
430	142	371	362	480	384	361	114	321	2965
Par 4	Par 3	Par 4	Par 4	Par 5	Par 4	Par 4	Par 3	Par 4	Par 35

Malone

*I*t's hard to believe you could find such a beautiful golf course so close to the city of Belfast. Yet just a few miles from the city centre you will find Malone, an excellent course set on rolling parkland with mature trees and a picturesque lake. It's a place where you would happily have a picnic on a fine summer's day.

Malone has been the venue for many tournaments over the years, including the Irish Amateur Championship, the Irish Professional Championship and the Irish Ladies Amateur Championship. As recently as 1994 it hosted the Irish Senior Masters, won by Tommy Horton. It's fitting that these tournaments have been played over this course, because Malone is a good test of golf.

Although the course only measures 6,599 yards to a par of 71, it will demand your best game to play to your handicap. You'll find a good mix of long and short holes. For example there are par-4s of 468 yards (the 7th) and 425-yards (the 18th). However, there are also par-4s that measure as little as 309-yards (the 16th), 366-yards (the 8th) and 365-yards (the 9th). Don't think the shorter ones are easier than the longer though, for they demand accuracy and a deft touch.

Best hole on the course is the delightful little par-3, 15th. This hole only stretches 132-yards, a mere flick for most. However, it's a flick that has to be played across a beautiful lake. Many good scores have been ruined by the sight of the lake's shimmering surface.

The same lake comes into play on the 18th, as it lies on the right hand side of the par-4, finishing hole. You'll need an accurate tee shot and an equally accurate approach to conquer a hole that is one of the better closing holes in parkland golf.

COURSE INFORMATION & FACILITIES

 Malone Golf Club
240 Upper Malone Road, Dunmurry, Belfast.

Club Manager: Nick Agate.
Tel: 01232-612758. Fax: 01232-431394.

Golf Professional Tel: 01232-614917.

Green Fees:
Weekdays – £32. Weekends & Wednesdays: £37.
Restrictions apply.

CARD OF THE COURSE – PAR 71

1	2	3	4	5	6	7	8	9	Out
382	505	522	158	440	195	468	366	365	3401
Par 4	Par 5	Par 5	Par 3	Par 4	Par 3	Par 4	Par 4	Par 4	Par 36

10	11	12	13	14	15	16	17	18	In
404	394	193	397	419	132	309	525	425	3198
Par 4	Par 4	Par 3	Par 4	Par 4	Par 3	Par 4	Par 5	Par 4	Par 35

HOW TO GET THERE

‹lmoral (A55) exit from M1 –
‹low signs for the Outer Ring
‹d Newcastle. At Malone
‹undabout take Upper Malone
‹ad exit to Sir Thomas and
‹dy Dixon Park – Golf Club
opposite.

STRANGFORD ARMS
— HOTEL —

Clandeboye

*I*t would be hard to find a golf course more pleasing to the eye than Clandeboye when the gorse is in full bloom. Here you are treated to a dazzling sea of yellow on many holes; in fact, the gorse runs for approximately 100 yards down the first hole, elegantly foreshadowing what's to come.

There are two courses at Clandeboye, the Ava and the Dufferin. The latter is the longer course, and the one that gets most of the tournaments and high praise. So it should, it is a challenging test for all handicap levels. It plays to a par of 71, stretching to 6,500 yards, and has been considered good enough to have hosted the Irish Professional Championship twice.

The Dufferin offers good views of Belfast Lough. Given the difficulty of some of the holes, that's just as well, for eventually you may be glad you're at least walking around in pleasant surroundings.

Good holes include the 6th, known as Rathgill, a 521-yard, par-5 which calls for an important decision on the tee. A stream about 250 yards out lies waiting for a good tee shot. Only the longest of hitters will consider trying to fly the ball over the stream while average golfers may do well to take a fairway wood just in case they hit one out of the screws. Trees to the right do not help those of have a penchant for the right hand side of the golf course.

The 18th is a strong finishing hole at 433 yards, which often calls for more club on the approach shot than seems the case.

While the Ava is some 800 or so yards shorter than its big brother, don't think it's a pushover. It isn't. Playing to your handicap is harder than you think on this little beauty.

COURSE INFORMATION & FACILITIES

Clandeboye Golf Club
51 Tower Road, Conlig,
Newtownards, Co. Down.

General Manager: William Donald.
Tel: 01247-27167. Fax: 01247-473711.

Golf Professional Tel: 01247-271750.

Green Fees:
Weekdays – (Dufferin) IR£25 (Ava) IR£20.
Weekends – (Dufferin) IR£15. (Ava) IR£15. After 3pm.

CARD OF THE COURSE – PAR 71

1	2	3	4	5	6	7	8	9	Out
388	172	417	389	183	521	360	452	392	3274
Par 4	Par 3	Par 4	Par 4	Par 3	Par 5	Par 4	Par 4	Par 4	Par 35

10	11	12	13	14	15	16	17	18	In
415	153	490	360	167	445	392	375	433	3230
Par 4	Par 3	Par 5	Par 4	Par 3	Par 5	Par 4	Par 4	Par 4	Par 36

HOW TO GET THERE

ual carriageway from Belfast
 Bangor (past Belfast City
rport), opposite Bangor
 emetery take Rathgael Road,
 roundabout take
 st exit right to
 ewtownards.

CLANDEBOYE LODGE
——HOTEL——

*A haven between country and coast,
past and present . . .*

In its idyllic setting the Clandeboye Lodge offers you a haven of tranquillity and luxury – whether you're staying on business or enjoying a sporting or leisure break. Each of our 43 luxury bedrooms is fully en suite and features direct-dial telephone with voicemail messaging, fax/modem point and satellite television. A trouser press and courtesy tray add a further touch of comfort and convenience.

In addition to golf, the area lends itself to all kinds of activity and leisure breaks. For guests wishing to explore further afield at their own pace, mountain bikes are available.

*HOLDER OF THREE RAC MERIT AWARDS:
FOR COMFORT, HOSPITALITY AND RESTAURANT*
Named Consort Hotels Group NI Regional Hotel of the Year 1997
10 Estate Road, Clandeboye, Bangor, Co. Down BT19 1UR
Tel: (01247) 852500   Fax: (01247) 852772

Belvoir Park

*T*his Belfast course was given the best start possible in life – it was designed by the inimitable Harry Colt.

Colt is responsible for many great layouts throughout the British Isles and around the world, including Swinley Forest, Sunningdale's New Course, Wentworth, The Eden Course at St Andrews, St George's Hill, Royal Portrush – he even had a hand in Pine Valley, recognised as the world's best. He didn't disappoint at Belvoir Park.

Harry Bradshaw once called Belvoir Park "the finest inland course I've ever played on." Mind you he could afford to be generous in his praise – he had just won the 1949 Irish Open Championship held here.

Four years later, the championship came back to Belvoir. This time it was won by Eric Brown. The Scottish Ryder Cup star holed in one at the long, par-3 16th on his way to

victory. You may not ace the 16th, nor any of the other four par-3s, but you will remember them later. The fourth is a 192-yard tester surrounded by trees, so it pays to hit the green. Fourteen is a cracker, as they would say in Ireland, calling for a medium iron over a big hollow to a raised green.

While the par-3s remain in the mind, don't think the par-4s and 5s are a pushover. They're not. You'll find a good mix of long holes, too.

Belvoir Park is a horticulturists delight, with a variety of different types of trees and bushes, including larch, fir, pine and cypress, to name only a few of the variety.

Sadly, Belvoir Park has faded somewhat into obscurity due to the troubles that have plagued this part of Ireland. Too bad, because this Colt gem should be on everyone's 'must play' list.

HOW TO GET THERE

…iles south from city
…tre. A24 to Newcastle.
…rance to golf club off
…urch Road,
…wtownbreda,
…traffic lights
…posite
…nsburys.

Belvoir Park
Golf Club

COURSE INFORMATION & FACILITIES

Belvoir Park Golf Club
73 Church Road,
Newtownbreda, Belfast.

Secretary/Manager: Kenneth H. Graham.
Tel: 01232-491693. Fax: 01232-646113.

Golf Professional Tel: 01232-646714.

Green Fees:
Weekdays – £33. Weekends (not Sat.) – £38.
Weekdays (day) – £33. Weekends (day) – £38.

CARD OF THE COURSE – PAR 72

1	2	3	4	5	6	7	8	9	Out
278	406	435	192	509	390	439	137	488	3274
Par 4	Par 4	Par 4	Par 3	Par 5	Par 4	Par 4	Par 3	Par 5	Par 36

10	11	12	13	14	15	16	17	18	In
476	179	463	402	175	497	204	449	397	3242
Par 5	Par 3	Par 4	Par 4	Par 3	Par 5	Par 3	Par 4	Par 4	Par 35

Ballycastle

Ballycastle belongs to one of the most glorious stretches of linksland in all of Ireland. This is a course that along with Royal Portrush, Portstewart and Castlerock comprises four of the most natural links course you are ever likely to find so close together.

It is isn't surprising that the four are the venues for the Black Bush Causeway Coast tournament played every June, a tournament that is usually oversubscribed due to its popularity.

Ballycastle may be the shortest of the four courses at just over 5,600 yards, but it is still fun to play nevertheless. True it won't really tax your game, but then it's the perfect course to play after tackling its other three illustrious neighbours. Indeed, you might want to start her first to hone your game before taking on the rigours of Royal Portrush. Ballycastle is a good introduction to links golf on the Antrim Coast. And if the wind is blowing, as it usually does, then you may not find Ballycastle as easy it appears on the card.

Two rivers, the Margy and the Carey, provide natural hazards over the opening five holes. The sixth and ninth are played along beside the sea, while holes 11 to 17 are played over an upland area that provides fantastic views of Ballycastle Bay, Rathlin Island and, on a clear day, even Scotland's famous Mull of Kintyre.

Your wedge and short irons will get a good workout at Ballycastle, as will your putter over the undulating greens.

Not championship golf, but good holiday fun stuff.

n the A2, between Portrush
d Cushendall.

Ballycastle
Golf Club

COURSE INFORMATION & FACILITIES

Ballycastle Golf Club
Cushendall Road, Ballycastle,
Co. Antrim.

Secretary: Mr. H. A. Fraser.
Tel: 012657-62536. Fax: 012657-69909.

Golf Professional Tel: 012657-62506.

Green Fees:
Weekdays – £18. Weekends – £25.
Some restrictions apply.

CARD OF THE COURSE – PAR 71

1	2	3	4	5	6	7	8	9	Out
482	339	151	395	252	258	385	301	335	2898
Par 5	Par 4	Par 3	Par 4	Par 4	Par 4	Par 4	Par 4	Par 4	Par 36

10	11	12	13	14	15	16	17	18	In
105	320	484	138	352	380	280	179	493	2731
Par 3	Par 4	Par 5	Par 3	Par 4	Par 4	Par 4	Par 3	Par 5	Par 35

Castlerock

Not far from the glorious links of Royal Portrush lies a gem of course where the River Bann enters the Atlantic Ocean.

Castlerock Golf Club was founded back in 1901, when it was established as a nine hole layout. The club expanded the course to 18 holes in 1908, calling upon Ben Sayers to create a golf course worthy enough to sit near Portrush. Sayers is better known as a clubmaker, but the North Berwick man could also play. For example, he participated in every Open Championship between 1880 and 1923, finishing second in 1888, third in 1889 and fifth in 1894.

While Sayers gave the game of golf clubs with names like the Jigger, the Benny and the Dreadnought, perhaps his best contribution is the links at Castlerock, six miles from Coleraine.

Good greens are the order of the day at Castlerock. In the height of summer, when the course is hard and dry, the greens can be treacherously quick. Given that you often have to bounce the ball in on the approach shot, getting close to the flags calls for a delicate touch.

The best known hole at Castlerock is the fourth, called Leg o' Mutton, a 200-yard, par-3 with a railway line to the right, a burn on the left and a raised green. Three here is a good score as this is a green that is hard to hold.

Castlerock varies from the norm in that it has five par-5s, four par-3s, and nine par-4s, meaning that it plays to a par of 73.

Changes to Sayers' layout were made by Harry Colt in 1925, and by Eddie Hackett in the 60s.

miles west of Coleraine, on
e A2.

Castlerock
Golf Club

COURSE INFORMATION & FACILITIES

Castlerock Golf Club
65 Circular Road, Castlerock,
Co. Londonderry.

Secretary: R. G. McBride
Tel: 01265-848314. Fax: 01265-848314.

Golf Professional Tel: 01265-848314.

Green Fees:
Weekdays – £20. Weekends – £30.
Weekdays (day) – £30. Weekends (day) – N/A.

CARD OF THE COURSE – PAR 72									
1	2	3	4	5	6	7	8	9	Out
348	375	509	200	477	347	409	411	200	3276
Par 4	Par 4	Par 5	Par 3	Par 5	Par 4	Par 4	Par 4	Par 3	Par 36
10	11	12	13	14	15	16	17	18	In
391	509	430	379	192	518	157	493	342	3411
Par 4	Par 5	Par 4	Par 4	Par 3	Par 5	Par 3	Par 5	Par 4	Par 37

Royal Portrush

Ask European Tour pro Darren Clarke to reveal his favourite golf and he'll say Royal Portrush without hesitation. In fact, he likes it so much he is a fully paid up member.

Royal Portrush was good enough to stage the only British Open Championship to be held off mainland Britain. The year was 1951, and England's eccentric Max Faulkner lifted the trophy.

Portrush was founded in 1888 and became Royal Portrush in 1893, with King Edward VII as its patron. It wasn't long before it attracted the attention of the game's best players. Portrush holds the distinction of hosting the first professional event in Ireland. In 1895 Sandy Herd, Portrush's first professional, defeated the legendary Harry Vardon over those glorious links.

Portrush calls for accurate driving most of the time, but especially when the rough is up. Miss the fairway and you'll be happy just to get the ball in play. Do it too often and you'll struggle to come close to your handicap.

The are plenty of good holes on the Dunluce course – in fact it could be argued that there isn't a bad hole on the course. However, of all the holes you play at Portrush, the 14th is the one that will stick in your mind. This is a 210-yard, par-3 that is known as Calamity. Stand on the tee looking at the green and you will know why. It calls for an accurate long iron or wood shot that must not go right. To slice or push the ball will earn you an almost sure double bogey, because the links land falls off down a steep slope towards the Valley course. Don't be ashamed of taking a four at this hole – threes are as rare as an unfriendly Irishman.

Don't skip the Valley Course when you go to Portrush. It may not be as good as the Dunluce, but it's a terrific links course and a joy to play.

COURSE INFORMATION & FACILITIES

Royal Portrush Golf Club
Dunluce Road, Portrush,
Co. Antrim.

Secretary/Manager: Wilma Erskine.
Tel: 01265-822311. Fax: 01265-823139.

Golf Professional Tel: 01265-823335.

Green Fees:
Weekdays – £50. Weekends – £60. (per round)
Letter of introduction required.

CARD OF THE COURSE – PAR 72

1	2	3	4	5	6	7	8	9	Out
392	505	155	457	384	189	431	384	475	3372
Par 4	Par 5	Par 3	Par 4	Par 4	Par 3	Par 4	Par 4	Par 5	Par 36

10	11	12	13	14	15	16	17	18	In
478	170	392	386	210	365	428	548	469	3446
Par 5	Par 3	Par 4	Par 4	Par 3	Par 4	Par 4	Par 5	Par 4	Par 36

HOW TO GET THERE

rom Belfast take M2 North,
urn on to A26, follow to
ortrush. Links can be seen
s you enter town.

Royal Portrush
Golf Club

Portstewart

*I*t's a claim that is often made, and one that won't be contested here – Portstewart has the best opening hole in Irish golf. Well, here's a little secret – it just might be the best opening hole in all of golf.

The first at Portstewart is legendary. Played from a high tee that affords wonderful views of nearby Donegal, the tee shot has to be played to a fairway well below you that doglegs right. You can try to cut the corner as much as possible, hitting as close to the line of the dogleg as possible. Achieve that and you will have a medium iron to the green. Slice or push the shot and you won't see the putting surface.

There used to be a sense that the first at Portstewart was something of a cheat. You played a great hole only to turn inland to holes that were good but didn't come anywhere near the first in terms of quality.

That is no longer the case.

The seven new holes built in 1990 over a wonderful stretch of duneland changed Portstewart for the better. Now there is no sense of letdown when you get to the next tee, or the next, or the next...

Holes two through eight appear as though they have been there for a hundred years, rather than as a late addition to the course. They are formidable as well. Get through this stretch of holes playing to your handicap and you'll have a chance to do well at Portstewart.

The Strand Course is the layout described above, and it stretches to just under 6,800 yards. It's one of the best in Ireland but there is also the Old Course if you want to hone your game before tackling the main course. It measures about 4,700 yards. It won't overly tax you, but it's popular and fun to play.

COURSE INFORMATION & FACILITIES

Portstewart Golf Club
117 Strand Road,
Portstewart.

Manager: Michael Moss.
Tel: 01265 832015. Fax: 01265 834097.

Golf Professional Tel: 01265 832601.

Green Fees:
Weekdays – £35. Weekends – £50.
Weekdays (day) – £50.
Time restrictions apply.

CARD OF THE COURSE – PAR 72

1	2	3	4	5	6	7	8	9	Out
425	366	207	535	456	140	511	384	352	3376
Par 4	Par 4	Par 3	Par 5	Par 4	Par 3	Par 5	Par 4	Par 4	Par 36
10	11	12	13	14	15	16	17	18	In
393	370	166	500	485	169	422	434	464	3403
Par 4	Par 4	Par 3	Par 5	Par 5	Par 3	Par 4	Par 4	Par 4	Par 36

HOW TO GET THERE

ollow signs for Portstewart –
nce there follow signs for
rand Beach. Golf Club is
cated on left overlooking
e beach.

North West

The North West

*T*he hauntingly beautiful county of Donegal, up in the left hand corner of the emerald isle, is a place not on many golfer's maps. That's a pity, for there is great golf to be found there. More importantly, it is a landscape you could easily fall in love with. There are many areas of Ireland that make you feel as if you're the only person in the whole of the island, nowhere gives you this sense of isolation more than Donegal. Not surprisingly there are times when you can go to this region, play its golf courses and find no one else on the course. Play almost any course in the county and you will experience golf in its most primitive state. For the most part it is links golf you will find in this remote region. If you're after manicured fairways and artificial conditions, then the courses of Donegal are not for you. If you're after golf the way it was meant to be played, then this is the place for you. The best courses in the region are to be found at Murvagh, near Donegal town, and at Ballyliffin in the far north of the county. These are links courses par excellence. Ballyliffin offers two links courses which are totally different. The Old Course at Ballyliffin has to be played by anyone interested in traditional golf. Here you will find fairways that ripple and roll. That is obvious from the first tee. The opening hole is called 'The Mounds' and that is exactly what the fairway consists of, a series of mounds that can throw the ball of at all sorts of strange angles. That sets the scene for the entire round, and hole after hole seems to offer up the whole range of features you expect to find on links courses. If the Old Course at Ballyliffin is a traditional links course that reminds you of the way golf was meant to be played, then the new Glashedy Links course is everything a championship layout should be. While the new is fairly short by modern standards, the new course is a big golf course in every sense of the word. You need to hit the ball a long way if you want to play off the back tees on the Glashedy Links. That's not usually the case for golf in Donegal, for the courses tend to be on the short side by modern standards.

That's normally not such a bad thing given that the wind is ever present. However, one course that would never be called short is Murvagh. This is a course that looks as if it was laid down a 100 years ago. In fact, it's one of the newer courses in the area. Play it from the back tees at your peril, because this is a course that includes all the hallmarks of links golf. Indeed, traditional links golf is what you will find in Donegal. From Northwest to Rosapenna, from Narin and Portnoo to Portsalon, everywhere you will find traditional seaside courses in some of the most hauntingly beautiful scenery.

BALLYLIFFIN
NORTH WEST
PORTSALON
ROSAPENNA
CRUIT ISLAND
NARIN & PORTNOO
DONEGAL

BUNDORAN
COUNTY SLIGO
ENNISCRONE
CARNE
WESTPORT
CONNEMARA

Ballyliffin

Ballyliffin is the most northerly links in Ireland, situated away up in Donegal near Malin Head. In fact, when you first arrive there, you're struck with one immediate thought - who the hell would come all the way up here to play golf? Well, Nick Faldo for one.

Like Watson at Ballybunion, Faldo fell in love with Ballyliffin the moment he saw it. Indeed, so much was he enthralled with the place that he offered to buy the entire complex.

See Ballyliffin for the first time and you'll know why Faldo wanted to buy the place.

There are two courses at Ballyliffin - the Old Course and the new Glashedy Links. The truth is the Old Course was always a bona fide "hidden gem" - still is - now it's the perfect compliment to what is one of the best ever designed links courses in the British Isles.

Pat Ruddy is the architect of the Glashedy course, a layout that takes its name from the giant rocky island that sits just offshore. Like the island, the eponymous golf course is formidable. This a man sized links which calls for every part of your game to be on song. Or else forget about beating your handicap.

If the Glashedy Links is an out and out challenge, then the Old Course is a unique experience. Here's a links course that's as natural as you will find anywhere. The first hole is called the mounds because thats what the surface of the fairway looks like. No gently undulating fairways here. These fairways ripple and roll, throwing the ball off at improbable angles even on the most perfectly struck tee shot. You won't find much of the hand of man on this course, just land that god presented to the architect. Wonderful.

COURSE INFORMATION & FACILITIES

Ballyliffin Golf Club
Ballyliffin,
Co. Donegal.

Marketing Convenor:
Cecil Doherty.
Tel: 077-76119. Fax: 077-76672.

Green Fees:
Weekdays – IR£22. Weekends – IR£27.

CARD OF THE COURSE – PAR 72

1	2	3	4	5	6	7	8	9	Out
426	432	428	479	177	361	174	422	382	3281
Par 4	Par 4	Par 4	Par 5	Par 3	Par 4	Par 3	Par 4	Par 4	Par 35

10	11	12	13	14	15	16	17	18	In
397	419	448	572	159	440	426	549	411	3821
Par 4	Par 4	Par 4	Par 5	Par 3	Par 4	Par 4	Par 5	Par 4	Par 37

HOW TO GET THERE

...avelling from Belfast (and ...erry) cross the Foyle Bridge ...d take the A2 towards ...oville, turning off for ...arndonagh at Quigleys ...oint/Carrowkeel. Ballyliffin ...6 miles from ...arndonagh.

35

North West

Northwest Golf Club will never host the Irish Open, or the Irish Amateur Championship for that matter. At just a little over 6,200 yards it isn't considered long enough to stage a tournament of note. Don't be fooled into thinking it's an easy course, though – it isn't.

Sure there are short holes at Northwest. Sure it only plays to a par of 69. Don't let looks deceive you, however. Northwest is a links course that can make you feel you play to a higher handicap than the one you showed up with. You'll realise that as you stand on the first tee looking at a tough par-4 that measures 440-yards. Making four at the first is no easy task, even for good players.

This is a truly natural little links course hard by the Atlantic Ocean. Not surprisingly, the Atlantic's capricious winds play a big part in how well you score. On a calm day you can score very well if your swing is on song. On a windy day you will realise why Northwest is not to be taken lightly.

At Northwest you will find par-4s ranging from 343-yards (the 4th), to 443-yards (the 12th), a definite drive and long iron hole for most players. You will find only two par-5s on the layout and five par-3s. Shortest of the par-3s is the 16th, which stretches to only 93-yards. However, it is surrounded by sand so hitting the green is imperative.

Northwest is situated in County Donegal only 12 miles north of Londonderry and about two miles south of Buncrana. It's a popular holiday spot in the summer so make sure you phone ahead in the months of July and August.

COURSE INFORMATION & FACILITIES

North West Golf Club
Lisfannon, Fahan,
Co. Donegal.

Hon. Secretary: Tom Crossan.
Tel: 077-61027. Fax: 077-63280.

Golf Professional Tel: 077-61715.

Green Fees:
Weekdays – IR£12. Weekends – IR£17.
Weekdays (day) – IR£120. Weekends (day) – IR£17.

CARD OF THE COURSE - PAR 70

1	2	3	4	5	6	7	8	9	Out
440	346	162	343	407	358	424	139	524	3143
Par 4	Par 4	Par 3	Par 4	Par 4	Par 4	Par 4	Par 3	Par 5	Par 35

10	11	12	13	14	15	16	17	18	In
386	358	443	177	349	370	93	407	513	3096
Par 4	Par 4	Par 4	Par 3	Par 4	Par 4	Par 3	Par 4	Par 5	Par 35

HOW TO GET THERE

mile from Buncrana on
ain Derry to Buncrana
ɔad.

North West Golf Club

Lake of Shadows Hotel

For centuries the elegant Victorian building of The Lake of Shadows Hotel has been sheltered under the rolling Donegal hills, overlooking Lough Swilly

A 23 bedroom family-run hotel where the homely atmosphere and friendly welcome reflect the gracious age in which the hotel was built. All bedrooms have en suite facilities, TV, telephone and tea/coffee making facilities. Excellent cuisine is served in the elegant, intimate dinning room, while the banqueting room can facilitate up to 300 people in the most pleasing surroundings. The Lake of Shadows bar is a popular rendezvous for locals and visitors and there is a regular programme of entertainment throughout the year. Visitors can use their stay at the Hotel as a focal point from which to discover the many interesting sides of the North West of Ireland – scenery, history, arts and crafts, wildlife, something to cater for everyone.

GRIANAN PARK, BUNCRANA, CO. DONEGAL, IRELAND
(Code from NI & UK 00353) Tel: 077 61005/077 61902 Fax: 077 62131

37

Portsalon

*F*or years visiting golfers came to Ireland and played the great courses on the Antrim Coast, went to the west of the Island and marvelled at Ballybunion and Lahinch, then went to Dublin and played Portmarnock, perhaps Royal Dublin, a few others and then went home. They never thought about exploring the Northwest corner of the Emerald Isle.

Golfers still largely ignore the beautiful county of Donegal. That's a pity because there is good golf to be found there.

Portsalon is one of those good golf courses in Donegal that doesn't get near the number of visitors it would do if it were located near Dublin, Killarney, Cork or Belfast. Like other courses in the region – Northwest, Rosapenna, Ballyliffin, Murvagh – Portsalon is a truly natural links, most of which is set in glorious duneland beside the Atlantic Ocean.

Established in 1890, Portsalon was in danger of virtual extinction until it was purchased by the members in 1986. Since then the course has made something of a comeback, with better care and attention given to what is a superb links.

The course only measures just under 6,000 yards to a par of 69, but like all the golf courses in Donegal, some days the scorecard lies – a yardage chart at Portsalon on a windy day would be a complete waste of time. Here you basically have to rely on instinct when it comes to club selection. Those able to overcome their machismo and hit a 5-iron 120-yards, or a 9-iron 170-yards, will succeed at Portsalon.

Arguably the most memorable hole on the course is the 431-yard, par-4, 13th hole. It has been dubbed Matterhorn because an odd pointed rock formation has to be negotiated on the second shot.

COURSE INFORMATION & FACILITIES

Portsalon Golf Club
Portsalon,
Co. Donegal.

Secretary: Cathal Toland.
Tel: 074-59459. Fax: 074-59459.

Green Fees per 18 holes:
Weekdays – IR£12. Weekends – IR£15.
Weekdays (day) – IR£12. Weekends (day) – IR£15.

CARD OF THE COURSE – PAR 69

1	2	3	4	5	6	7	8	9	Out
365	196	356	344	208	354	514	174	317	2828
Par 4	Par 3	Par 4	Par 4	Par 3	Par 4	Par 5	Par 3	Par 4	Par 34

10	11	12	13	14	15	16	17	18	In
351	323	186	431	155	388	285	526	405	3050
Par 4	Par 4	Par 3	Par 4	Par 3	Par 4	Par 4	Par 5	Par 4	Par 35

HOW TO GET THERE

) miles north of Letterkenny.

Portsalon Golf Club

Rosapenna

When Frank Casey bought the Rosapenna hotel in 1981, the golf course was thrown in with the deal. For £500,000 Casey not only bought a good hotel overlooking the wild Atlantic Ocean, but purchased hundreds of acres of the finest duneland you could ever come across. Casey's acquisition also saved a course that was fading slowly and sadly into extinction.

Rosapenna was given the best possible start in life. This remote Donegal course was conceived by Old Tom Morris. Later it was remodelled at different times by James Braid and Harry Vardon. Some courses are lucky enough to have one Open Champion involved in their evolution, Rosapenna had three.

Unfortunately the trio did not have access to modern equipment, and so wild were the dunes at Rosapenna that only 10 holes could be constructed on proper linksland before the course had to move inland. The holes in the dunes just got you into the rhythm of links golf before the final eight left you with the feeling that you had actually played two courses. In the old days you had. Modern technology has ensured that you now play proper links golf when you go to Rosapenna.

New holes have been created in the dunes to rival the first 10 holes. Casey called in another great architect. Although not an Open Champion, Eddie Hackett's work on numerous courses, links and otherwise, around Ireland made him the obvious choice to add to the work of Morris, Braid and Vardon. Rosapenna is now an excellent 27 hole complex that shouldn't be missed on any trip to Donegal.

What's more, the hotel serves excellent seafood. The Lobster is reason enough to visit the Rosapenna Hotel - the golf just happens to be a mouth-watering bonus.

COURSE INFORMATION & FACILITIES

Rosapenna Golf Club
Downings,
Co. Donegal.

Director: Frank T. Casey.
Tel: 074-55128.

Golf Professional Tel: 074-55128.

Green Fees:
Weekdays – IR£18. Weekends – IR£20.
Weekdays (day) – IR£30. Weekends (day) – IR£35.

CARD OF THE COURSE – PAR 70

1	2	3	4	5	6	7	8	9	Out
298	428	446	386	255	167	367	485	185	3017
Par 4	Par 4	Par 4	Par 4	Par 4	Par 3	Par 4	Par 5	Par 3	Par 35

10	11	12	13	14	15	16	17	18	In
543	427	342	455	128	418	216	358	367	3254
Par 5	Par 4	Par 4	Par 4	Par 3	Par 4	Par 3	Par 4	Par 4	Par 35

HOW TO GET THERE

Miles North of Letterkenny.

Rosapenna
Golf Club

Cruit Island

Cruit Island will never host a major professional championship, nor will it even host any of the top amateurs. You see, it's only a nine hole course, but my there's enough fun at Cruit to make you think you're playing a regular 18-holer.

Cruit Island is hard to find, but if you can make your way to Dungloe then you are not far away. Cruit Island is located another five miles to the north, at Kincasslagh.

You actually do cross a little bridge that spans the Atlantic to get to the island, which is a busy holiday spot in summer. Go there out of season and you're likely to have the course all to yourself. Don't be surprised if there's no one there to take the green fee. There is no professional at Cruit, nor is there a pro shop of sorts, just a simple club house that is normally closed in winter.

Don't worry if the place is deserted, simply find the honesty box and deposit your money. Then enjoy Cruit for all its worth.

This is links golf as primitive as it comes. The wild Atlantic is never very far away, and usually provides a magnificent backdrop for many shots you have to play. You actually play the nine hole loop twice to make up your 18 holes, playing the second time from different tees.

The yardage for the total 18 is just over 5,297 yards, so it's not really going to provide a stern test. Mind you, the wind is strong in this exposed part of Donegal, so you may not actually bring it to its knees. But don't worry about your score, let the fresh wind off the Atlantic blow through your hair and enjoy the scenery. Golf was always meant to be fun, and that's what you'll have at Cruit Island.

COURSE INFORMATION & FACILITIES

Cruit Island Golf Club
Cruit Island, Kincasslagh,
Letterkenny, Co. Donegal.

Secretary:
Dermot Devenney.
Tel: 075-48151.

Green Fees:
Weekdays – IR£7.   Weekends – IR£10.
Weekdays (Day) – IR£7.   Weekends (Day) – IR£10.

CARD OF THE COURSE (metres) – PAR 68

1	2	3	4	5	6	7	8	9	Out
282	386	283	313	256	127	273	188	285	2393
Par 4	Par 4	Par 4	Par 4	Par 4	Par 3	Par 4	Par 3	Par 4	Par 34

10	11	12	13	14	15	16	17	18	In
370	386	283	313	256	121	265	188	285	2467
Par 4	Par 4	Par 3	Par 5	Par 4	Par 3	Par 4	Par 3	Par 4	Par 34

HOW TO GET THERE

...cent to Donegal International Airport.
...se situated on an Island accessible by a
...ge only. Roadway opposite to
...iel O Donnells Viking House Hotel.
...rox. 5 miles north of Dungloe
...Burtonport.

Cruit Island
Golf Club

Narin & Portnoo

Play the seaside courses in Donegal and you'll soon find there's nowhere to hide from the wind. That's especially true at the delightfully named Narin and Portnoo.

It's not a long course, but the wind can sometimes make it feel like a walk in purgatory, as if the devil was blowing at you through a straw. Holes that would normally call for a drive and pitch sometimes ask you to play a driver and 2-iron only to see the ball come up short.

Narin and Portnoo only measures 5,800 yards to a par of 69, but it will feel like 7,800 on some days. This is a totally natural course that seems to jut out into the Atlantic Ocean. Indeed the holes closest to the sea are the best on the course, although they can be a nightmare when the wind is howling. And here's the rub: you very seldom get a calm day in this part of Donegal.

Get your iron play in shape before you play golf in this remote part of Donegal, fo Narin and Portnoo has six par-3s. There are some crackers, as the Irish would say, but best of the bunch may be the 16th. Called High Altar, the hole only measures about 120-yards. However you have to play to a green that drops off on all sides. In a gale you can be hitting a wood.

A word of warning – if the secretary says it's just a gentle breeze, sit in the clubhouse and enjoy a pint of the black stuff. There's lots of time for golf in Donegal.

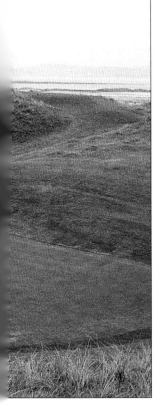

COURSE INFORMATION & FACILITIES

Narin & Portnoo Golf Club
Narin, Portnoo,
Co. Donegal.

Secretary: Enda Bonner.
Tel: 074-24668. Fax: 074-25185.

Golf Professional Tel: 075-45107.

Green Fees:
Weekdays – IR£13. Weekends – IR£16.
Weekdays (day) – IR£13. Weekends (day) – IR£16.
Weekends – booking only.

CARD OF THE COURSE (metres) – PAR 69

1	2	3	4	5	6	7	8	9	Out
289	450	171	416	356	187	292	130	294	2585
Par 4	Par 5	Par 3	Par 4	Par 4	Par 3	Par 4	Par 3	Par 4	Par 34

10	11	12	13	14	15	16	17	18	In
356	180	303	170	476	450	110	371	321	2737
Par 4	Par 3	Par 4	Par 3	Par 5	Par 5	Par 3	Par 4	Par 4	Par 35

HOW TO GET THERE

m Donegal town – follow
in road to Glenties for
miles, then road to
ngloe for 5 miles.
Mass take the road
Narin/Portnoo.

in & Portnoo
Golf Club

Donegal

*D*on't go to Donegal and miss Murvagh. Those were the words of Christy O'Connor Jnr. Now when such a famous Irish golfer gives you advice, it pays to listen.

Christy knows his stuff, for Murvagh is a true hidden gem. Play it and you'll be convinced it's been there for at least a 100 years. It hasn't – this cracking links course was only laid down in 1973.

The ubiquitous Eddie Hackett was responsible for Murvagh, and it's one of his best. This is a true links course that will test the best, especially from the back tees, where the course measures over 7,150 yards.

The first four holes don't really give you a taste of what's to come. Although they're good holes, they are played over land that can't really be called true links. Then comes the 5th.

Beginning with the 5th, you are into proper links country, in amongst the dunes. The hole is a beauty, too, a par-3 of 187 yards with a high green. To come up short of the fifth green is to roll back down into a collection of bunkers, from where par is virtually impossible.

Murvagh is man-sized golf. Although the outward nine is longer than the inward by more than two hundred yards, don't be fooled into thinking the back half will be easier.

Coming home you face one of the longest par-5s in Ireland. The 12th hole measures almost 600 yards and calls for three wood shots by most mortals. Then there's the 16th, which is a par-3 hole of 240 yards. Most accept a four here as a good score, that's how tough the hole is from the back.

Play Murvagh from sensible tees unless you've got some sort of sadistic streak in you. And enjoy the fine views it offers of the Atlantic and the mountains of Donegal- they'll more than compensate for the troubles you'll be experiencing if you're playing from the back markers.

COURSE INFORMATION & FACILITIES

Donegal Golf Links
Murvagh, Laghey,
Co. Donegal.

Administrator: John Mcbride.
Tel: 073-34054. Fax: 073-34377.

Green Fees:
Weekdays – IR£17. Weekends – IR£22.50.
Weekdays (day) – IR£17. Weekends (day) – N/A.

CARD OF THE COURSE (metres) – PAR 73

1	2	3	4	5	6	7	8	9	Out
478	424	190	436	174	478	401	499	306	3386
Par 5	Par 4	Par 3	Par 4	Par 3	Par 5	Par 4	Par 5	Par 4	Par 37

10	11	12	13	14	15	16	17	18	In
320	365	547	145	501	370	219	323	365	3155
Par 4	Par 4	Par 5	Par 3	Par 5	Par 4	Par 3	Par 4	Par 4	Par 36

HOW TO GET THERE

f the N15, main
negal/Ballyshannon road.
niles from Donegal and
llyshannon.

Bundoran

Play this flat, basically featureless, links course and you will realise why Christy O'Connor was such a brilliant shotmaker. O'Connor, or Himself as he is oft referred to, was the professional at Bundoran during the 1950s. You have to be a good shotmaker at Bundoran, for when the wild winds off the Atlantic sweep across you need to manufacture shots to get the ball near the hole.

Bundoran dates back to 1894, when it was just a 9-hole course. It was extended in the 1920s, when Harry Vardon was brought in to make it a stiff test. That it is. The only problem was, Vardon wasn't given that much more room than what was allocated to the 9-hole course. As a result space is at a premium at Bundoran, so you're never very

far away from other golfers.

You won't find sand dunes at Bundoran, which makes the wind more of a factor here than at most seaside courses you are likely to play in Ireland. The length of the course is deceptively short, too. There is only one par-5, which comes as early as the second tee shot. At less than 6,300 yards to a par of 69, Bundoran looks a pushover on the card. Don't be fooled, it is anything but easy.

There are two par-3s of over 200 yards, the 217-yard 5th and the 237-yard 13th. Needless to say, making par on each of them isn't the easiest of propositions. Besides the par-3s, there four par-4s of over 400 yards, all on the back nine.

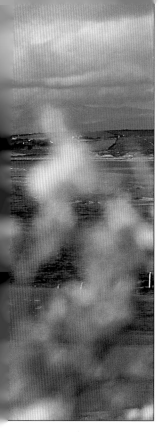

COURSE INFORMATION & FACILITIES

Bundoran Golf Club
Bundoran,
Co. Donegal.

Secretary/Manager: John McGagh.
Tel: 072-41302. Fax: 072-42014.

Golf Professional Tel: 072-41302.

Green Fees:
Weekdays – IR£16. Weekends – IR£18.
Booking essential.

CARD OF THE COURSE – PAR 69

1	2	3	4	5	6	7	8	9	Out
327	459	117	331	197	180	325	356	356	2648
Par 4	Par 5	Par 3	Par 4	Par 3	Par 3	Par 4	Par 4	Par 4	Par 34

10	11	12	13	14	15	16	17	18	In
364	384	316	212	366	390	142	453	324	2951
Par 4	Par 4	Par 4	Par 3	Par 4	Par 4	Par 3	Par 5	Par 4	Par 35

HOW TO GET THERE

miles north of Sligo on
ain Sligo/Derry Road.

County Sligo

*I*f you're going to play County Sligo, or Rosses Point as it's also known, then you might just want to consider brushing up on your knowledge of the verse of William Butler Yeats, Ireland's most famous poet.

The land around Sligo is Yeats' country. In fact, Ireland's best bard is buried nearby, within sight of Benbulben, the mountain that dominates the region and much of Yeats' poetry.

You may not appreciate poetry, but rest assured that Rosses Point will have you waxing lyrical after just one round.

This is a links course that has many fans. Tom Watson, Peter Alliss and Bernhard Langer, to name but a few, have all sung its praises. And no wonder, once you reach the fifth tee, you know you're on a special piece of links turf.

There are many courses in Ireland with great views, and Rosses Point is no exception. From as early as the third tee you are presented with stunning views of Drumcliffe Bay, the Atlantic Ocean, the Ox Mountains and Benbulben, Yeats' mountain.

Enjoy the views on the third, for after a bunkerless, medium iron par-3, the real test that is County Sligo begins at the 5th tee. This hole is called the Jump and is aptly named, for you jump from the high ground around the clubhouse down into true golfing country. This par-5 hole calls for a tee shot to be played from a clifftop tee to a fairway lying far below you. Now you're in true golfing country, playing among sand dunes, pot bunkers and elusive, undulating greens. Fabulous.

County Sligo is the venue for the West of Ireland Championship, a prestigious amateur event with many fine winners that dates back to 1924. Oh, and Harry Colt had a hand in the design of the course – that should be enough to have you packing your bags and heading for Sligo Town.

CARD OF THE COURSE (metres) – PAR 71

1	2	3	4	5	6	7	8	9	Out
347	278	457	150	438	387	385	374	153	2969
Par 4	Par 4	Par 5	Par 3	Par 5	Par 4	Par 4	Par 4	Par 3	Par 36

10	11	12	13	14	15	16	17	18	In
351	366	485	162	394	367	196	414	336	3071
Par 4	Par 4	Par 5	Par 3	Par 4	Par 4	Par 3	Par 4	Par 4	Par 35

HOW TO GET THERE

m north west of Sligo city
Rosses Point village.

Enniscrone

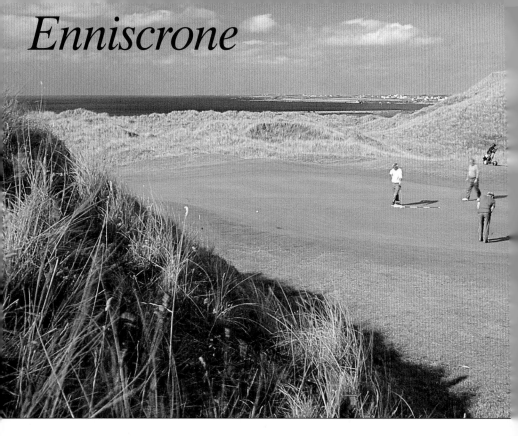

ind the Enniscrone Golf Club and you find another creation by Ireland's foremost architect. That's right, Enniscrone is the work of Eddie Hackett.

Take a tip – don't quit after the first two holes. That's the feeling as you walk the second fairway. "I was expecting an exciting links," you'll probably say to yourself, "yet here I am on the two most boring holes I've ever played." Persevere, please.

After the opening two par-5s, the course begins to grow on you, so much so that by the time you get into the back nine you've completely forgotten the opening duo.

Enniscrone proper basically starts at the par-3, 5th, a beautiful little one shotter of 170 yards set into the dunes. From here it is pretty well links golf all the way. The routing of the holes takes you into high sand hills, and from there back down to flattish

fairways only to go into the high duneland again, a veritable roller-coaster of a trek through thoroughly natural links land.

At just over 6,700 yards to a par of 72, Hackett doesn't ask you to hit your tee shots 300-yards. Indeed, this is a course average handicaps can play well, especially since there is a good variety of shortish par 4s. But remember, this is the west coast of Ireland. The Atlantic Ocean is nearby and will throw strong winds at the links. Play it on a calm day and you will have experienced something rare. Play it when there's a strong wind and it will feel like 7,400 yards.

Enniscrone has been gaining in reputation over the years. A new clubhouse built in 1992 at a cost of £250,000 has done much to enhance Enniscrone. This is a club that welcomes visitors with open arms.

CARD OF THE COURSE – PAR 72

1	2	3	4	5	6	7	8	9	Out
551	535	395	534	170	395	374	170	345	3469
Par 5	Par 5	Par 4	Par 5	Par 3	Par 4	Par 4	Par 35	Par 4	Par 37

10	11	12	13	14	15	16	17	18	In
350	427	540	202	368	412	403	149	400	3251
Par 4	Par 4	Par 5	Par 3	Par 4	Par 4	Par 4	Par 3	Par 4	Par 35

HOW TO GET THERE

km from Ballina.

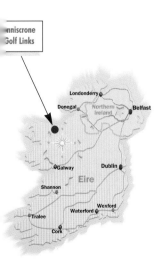

Enniscrone
Golf Links

Carne

You often get the sense of complete isolation playing in Ireland, as if you are playing at the end of the earth, as far from civilisation as possible. Nowhere in Ireland is this sense more profound than at Carne. The nearest town, Ballina, is 30 miles away.

Carne is about as far west as you can get on mainland Ireland. Any farther west and the Statue of Liberty would just about be visible. The course is situated on Mullet peninsula, on the edge of the Atlantic Ocean. Here you will find glorious views of Blacksod Bay and various islands out in the Atlantic.

Carne was built with one aim - to attract tourism. Those who have sampled its delights since the Eddie Hackett designed course was opened in 1993 have spread the word. Carne is worthy of trekking to this isolated part of County Mayo, and more golfers are doing so every year.

So natural is the linksland, that there is feeling the course has been here for years. The greens, in particular, seem to belong to the land, as if the golfing greats have been pacing them since the turn of the century.

Huge sand dunes are the order of the day at Carne, and many are used to elevate the tees. This means that on most holes you can see the trouble that lies ahead. That's not to say you will avoid it, for the wind plays a big part in how well you play this course. Pray you get a calm day, otherwise you'll struggle to match your handicap. Just as well it only measures just over 6,600 yards.

COURSE INFORMATION & FACILITIES

Carne Golf Links
Carne, Belmullet
Co. Mayo, Eire.

Director: Eamon Mangan.
Tel: 097-81124. Fax: 097-81477.

Green Fees:
Weekdays – IR£17. Weekends – IR£17.
Weekdays (day) – IR£17. Weekends (day) – IR£17.

CARD OF THE COURSE – PAR 72

1	2	3	4	5	6	7	8	9	Out
366	183	376	473	378	363	162	365	327	2993
Par 4	Par 3	Par 4	Par 5	Par 4	Par 4	Par 3	Par 4	Par 4	Par 35
10	11	12	13	14	15	16	17	18	In
465	332	271	482	133	366	154	399	495	3097
Par 5	Par 4	Par 4	Par 5	Par 3	Par 4	Par 3	Par 4	Par 5	Par 37

HOW TO GET THERE

59 to Belmullet

Carne
Golf Links

Westport

The delightful little town of Westport has been a magnet for visitors for years. People come here for a relaxing holiday, or to walk the rugged coastline, or trudge up a mountain to see the spot where St Patrick is said to have banished all the snakes from Ireland.

Croagh Patrick is the mountain in question, and every year thousands of worshippers ascend Ireland's Holy Mountain. This same mountain stands towering above the golf course at Westport, providing a unique backdrop.

A golf course is just what Westport needed to make it the ideal holiday destination in County Mayo, and Fred Hawtree has designed a course the town can be justifiably proud of.

Although the course sits by the sea, it is not a links course. This is basically pure parkland, with a good mixture of holes on lush terrain. Don't be lulled into a false sense of security by the opening nine, which are fairly straightforward. The course really comes into its own on the inward half.

Westport is long. From the back markers it stretches to 7,000 yards. That was long enough for the course to be selected as venue for the 1977 and 1985 Irish Amateur Close Championship, as well as the 1989 Irish Ladies Amateur Championship.

Although basically a parkland layout, Westport has one hole that wouldn't be out of place on any fine links course. The 580-yard, par-5, 15th is the hole in question, and it is simply stunning. It calls for a drive to be played over Clew Bay and then the hole bends round to the left back towards the water. Make par here from the back tees and you've had a result.

HOW TO GET THERE

5 miles from Westport town, on Newport Road. Turn on Newport Road after leaving Westport and continue for approximately miles.

Westport Golf Club

COURSE INFORMATION & FACILITIES

Westport Golf Club
Carrowholly, Westport,
Co. Mayo.

Secretary: Margaret Walsh.
Tel: 098-28262. Fax: 098-27217.

Golf Professional Tel: 098-28262.

Green Fees:
Weekdays – IR£18. Weekends – IR£22.50.
Time restrictions apply.

CARD OF THE COURSE – PAR 73

1	2	3	4	5	6	7	8	9	Out
348	343	162	501	356	453	524	468	202	3357
Par 4	Par 4	Par 3	Par 5	Par 4	Par 4	Par 5	Par 4	Par 3	Par 36

10	11	12	13	14	15	16	17	18	In
517	433	220	455	189	580	363	378	520	3655
Par 5	Par 4	Par 3	Par 4	Par 3	Par 5	Par 4	Par 4	Par 5	Par 37

Connemara

onnemara is another of those Irish courses where you feel as if you're at the very edge of civilisation. It's hard to believe there is a actually a golf course in this remote part of County Galway, yet here lies a fabulous links some five miles beyond the town of Clifden at Ballyconneely.

Eddie Hackett is responsible for this stunning course. Hackett designed the course in 1973, taking full advantage of the huge rocks which dot this landscape. Hackett was actually able to design the course without moving a rock, a tribute to his skill as a designer.

While this is a bona fide links, you won't find the type of sand dunes you normally expect. That means you are more at the mercy of the winds which whip over the course from the Atlantic Ocean. And, yes, there is always a wind.

Calm days at Connemara are rare indeed

You'll pray for a calm day when you look at the scorecard, for Connemara is a long golf course. Play it from the back if there is no wind or you're feeling macho, otherwise play from the forward tees. To give you an example, there are par-4s of 475-yards (8th), 443 yards (9th), 432 yards (10th) 451 yards (12th) and 452 yards (16th), plus the four par-5s measure 576-yards (7th, 523-yards (14th), 532-yards (17th), and 537-yards (18th).

Make sure you take advantage of the front nine, as it is about 300 yards shorter than the inward half, which is tough and commanding.

Connemara provides superb views of the Atlantic Ocean and an the imposing mountain range dubbed the Twelve Bens for obvious reasons.

COURSE INFORMATION & FACILITIES

Connemara Golf Club
Ballyconneely,
Co. Galway.

Secretary/Manager: John McLaughlin.
Tel: 095-23502/23602. Fax: 095-23662.

Green Fees:
May to Sept (inclusive) – IR£25.
Jan to April/Oct to Dec (inclusive) – IR£16.

CARD OF THE COURSE (metres) – PAR 72

1	2	3	4	5	6	7	8	9	Out
349	385	154	358	360	193	531	438	408	3176
Par 4	Par 4	Par 3	Par 4	Par 4	Par 3	Par 5	Par 4	Par 4	Par 35

10	11	12	13	14	15	16	17	18	In
398	171	416	196	483	367	417	491	496	3435
Par 4	Par 3	Par 4	Par 3	Par 5	Par 4	Par 4	Par 5	Par 5	Par 37

HOW TO GET THERE

)m Clifden, continue
ough Ballyconneely – after
t turning for Roundstone
d before the Pier, the Golf
ub will be found on
e right.

Connemara
Golf Club

South West

The South West

Ballybunion, Waterville Killarney, Tralee, Dooks. They're names that make you want to pack your clubs and head for Ireland, for the County of Kerry and the Southwest corner of the emerald isle. Golfers have been doing that for years, most making Killarney their base from which to explore Kerry and it's famous ring. The Ring of Kerry is one of the great drives in the world. It's a journey that takes you around a peninsula that offers simply the most glorious views to be found anywhere in the world. Keeping your eyes on the road will be no easy matter. For golfers the drive is even more memorable, for you have to drive out this way to get to Dooks and Waterville, two links courses worthy of even the most boring car journey, let alone this scenic route. The two courses couldn't differ more, Waterville is a true championship layout, while Dooks is one of Ireland's true gems. Waterville is a big golf course in every sense of the word, especially the back nine, which is the making of the course. On this loop you will encounter hole after challenging hole, culminating in a par-3 that is simply stunning. The tee of the par-3 17th is known as Mulcahy's Peak, after the man responsible for this fine links. The tee offers stunning views over the golf course, a spot Jack Mulcahy often visited to look over the land that would one day become one of the best links courses anywhere. If you have to play off forward tees on this hole, make sure you take a walk up to the top of the tee to have a look around. You may want to just sit there all day and soak in the scenery. Dooks is another course where you will want to soak up the atmosphere. It might not be a long course, but you'll be hard pressed to find one that is more fun to play. And even if you do play poorly, the views will more than compensate. The scenery is also one of the major pluses at Killarney Golf Club. Killarney's two courses are dominated by the Magilicuddy Reeks, the tallest mountains in Ireland. Between the courses and the slopes of the Reeks lies Lough Leane. There is no finer place to play golf on a sunny day. However, the most famous *ourse in this region is not known so much for its outstanding beauty as its utstanding golf course. Ballybunion is the course in question, and the Old Course there just has to be played at least once. Tom Watson is the man esponsible for Ballybunion's popularity with American golfers. Watson thinks 's one of the best courses anywhere in the world. He's right. Ballybunion is raditional links golf at its very best. Make Killarney your base when you visit Kerry. It's a town packed with good pubs and fine restaurants and lots of first lass accommodation. It's also quite handy for any golf course in the region.*

GALWAY
LAHINCH
DROMOLAND
LIMERICK
ADARE MANOR
BALLYBUNION
TRALEE
KILLARNEY

DOOKS
BEAUFORT
WATERVILLE
LEE VALLEY
OLD HEAD
CORK
FOTA ISLAND

Galway Bay

Christy O'Connor Jnr didn't need Peter McEvoy's help when he laid out the course that is Galway Bay Golf & Country Club. However, he didn't design all 18 holes. He called on the help of his famous uncle, Christy O'Connor Snr, allowing him to create one hole on his course. The result is the 176-yard, par-3 13th hole.

Chisty Jnr had always dreamt of designing a golf course in his home town. In fact, his eye had been on the land his course now occupies for some time prior to development. It's land that sits on the Galway Peninsula, with splendid views out over the Atlantic Ocean. As you can appreciate, the wind is often a factor at Galway Bay.

Although it has the Atlantic on three sides, Galway Bay is not a links course. You won't find high duneland here, or turf that is firm and fast. This is essentially a parkland course set beside the sea. However, like link courses you will find lots of bunkers. There isn't one green that is bunker free on the whole course.

Although it is quite open, Galway Bay is a stiff test of golf. It's a big course in every sense of the word, measuring close to 7,100 yards, par-72, with long par-4s and 5s. Three of the par-4s measure 457-yards (2nd), 446-yards (10th) and 477-yards (18th). Thankfull the par-3s are of sensible distance, ranging from 149-yards to 188-yards.

While not a links course, Galway Bay is nevertheless set in beautiful landscape. Christy and his uncle have done well to create a course that compliments the scenery But take a tip, play the course from sensible tees, unless you're a big hitter – that way you'll enjoy the walk.

COURSE INFORMATION & FACILITIES

Galway Bay Golf and Country Club Hotel
Renville, Oranmore,
Co. Galway.

Golf Director: Eamon Meagher.
Tel: 091-790-500. Fax: 091-792-510.

Golf Professional Tel: 091-790-503.

Green Fees:
Weekdays (May-Sept) – IR£30, (Oct-April) – IR£25.
Weekends (May-Sept) – IR£35, (Oct-April) – IR£30.

CARD OF THE COURSE (metres) – PAR 72

1	2	3	4	5	6	7	8	9	Out
486	362	370	136	323	434	126	386	374	2997
Par 5	Par 4	Par 4	Par 3	Par 4	Par 5	Par 3	Par 4	Par 4	Par 36

10	11	12	13	14	15	16	17	18	In
367	356	372	148	464	160	481	323	423	3094
Par 4	Par 4	Par 4	Par 3	Par 5	Par 3	Par 5	Par 4	Par 4	Par 36

HOW TO GET THERE

…8 Limerick to Galway.
…low signs for and go through
…anmore, take first on left, follow
…d for approx. 2 miles.

…Dublin to Galway. Follow signs
…and go through Oranmore,
…n right at church
…d follow road
…approx.
…niles.

Galway Bay
Golf Club

Lahinch

When a man of the calibre of Dr. Alister MacKenzie is responsible in the design of a course you are about to play, you know you are in for something special. The links of Lahinch are just that.

Aficionados will know that MacKenzie is the man who helped Bobby Jones create his dream course of Augusta National, that he is the man who designed, among others, Cypress Point and Royal Melbourne. Any course touched by MacKenzie is worth playing, and Lahinch is no different.

MacKenzie did not design the original Lahinch. Old Tom Morris did that in 1892. In 1907 Charles Gibson, the professional at Westward Ho!, made refinements before MacKenzie was hired in 1927 to make what is essentially the course you play today, albeit with later adjustments by John Burke and Donald Steel. Working with Old Tom's original design, MacKenzie transformed Lahinch, building holes in duneland previously thought too wild for golf.

While MacKenzie had strong views on golf course design, he knew good golf holes when he saw them. He did not touch two of Old Tom's holes, preferring to leave them as they were. The par-5, 5th hole and the par-3, 6th are the holes in question, holes called "Klondyke" and the "Dell" respectively. They would not be built today, for they both call for blind shots to greens tucked away in the Dunes. The Dell will remind you of Prestwick's famous par-3, 5th, the "Himalayas", as it too calls for a blind tee shot to be played over a high ridge. Old Tom would have known Prestwick's 5th very well.

MacKenzie has helped create a gem of a course at Lahinch, one that is traditional in every sense of the word. It's a magnificent test of golf, especially when the wind blows, as it usually does in this part of County Clare.

COURSE INFORMATION & FACILITIES

Lahinch Golf Club
Lahinch,
Co. Clare.

Secretary/Manager: Alan Reardon.
Tel: 065-81003. Fax: 065-81592.

Golf Professional:
Tel: 065-81592.

Green Fees (old course):
Weekdays – IR£40. Weekends – IR£40.
Weekdays (day) – IR£50. Weekends (day) – IR£50.

Letter of introduction required.

CARD OF THE COURSE – PAR 72

1	2	3	4	5	6	7	8	9	Out
343	455	135	380	435	137	350	318	322	2875
Par 4	Par 5	Par 3	Par 4	Par 5	Par 3	Par 4	Par 4	Par 4	Par 36

10	11	12	13	14	15	16	17	18	In
385	122	418	244	440	403	164	382	457	3015
Par 4	Par 3	Par 4	Par 4	Par 5	Par 4	Par 3	Par 4	Par 5	Par 36

HOW TO GET THERE

...m the town of Ennis, take
...N67 to Ennistymon and
...inch is two miles from
...nistymon
...the Sea.
...s well
...nposted.

Dromoland

A trend in Irish golf in the late 80s and early 90s has been for stately homes and castles with large tracts of land to construct golf courses on the property. The stately homes become first rate hotels and those who want to wine and dine in style can also include a round of two of golf. All very civilised indeed.

Adare Manor, The K-Club, Mount Juliet, to name only three, spring readily to mind. Dromoland Castle is another.

Dromoland Castle dates back to the 16th century, and for a long time was the ancestral home of the powerful O'Brien clan of County Clare, descendants of Brian Boru, the 10th century Irish King. The castle is very much in view from the golf course, indeed it provides a spectacular backdrop to the 140-yard, par-3, 7th hole. The course itself is of the parkland variety set out over rolling ground, with very few trees that come into play.

Water comes into play at Dromoland, as does a river, so make sure you are not wayward. The course won't call for you to hit every club in the bag, and at around 6,200 you don't need to be a long hitter. Make sure you concentrate from the very beginning, though, as the front nine is some 400 yards longer than the back. You'll need to be a good long iron or fairway wood player, too, as the outward half closes with a demanding 220-yard, par-3.

COURSE INFORMATION & FACILITIES

Dromoland Castle Golf & Country Club
Newmarket-on-Fergus,
Co. Clare.

Secretary/Golf Manager: John O'Halloran.
Tel: 061-368444/368144.
Fax: 061-368498/363355.

Green Fees:
Weekdays – IR£25. Weekends – IR£30.
Weekdays (day) – IR£25. Weekends (day) – IR£30.

CARD OF THE COURSE (metres) – PAR 71

1	2	3	4	5	6	7	8	9	Out
356	480	212	423	377	513	130	358	206	3055
Par 4	Par 5	Par 3	Par 4	Par 4	Par 5	Par 3	Par 4	Par 3	Par 35

10	11	12	13	14	15	16	17	18	In
268	440	317	110	358	257	347	153	414	2664
Par 4	Par 5	Par 4	Par 3	Par 4	Par 4	Par 4	Par 3	Par 5	Par 36

HOW TO GET THERE

m Shannon airport –
e N19, follow signs to
3 Newmarket-on-Fergus.
niles past village entrance,
) is on right.

noland Castle
Golf Club

Limerick

Golf has been played at Limerick Golf Club since 1891, when officers of the Scottish regiment the Black Watch introduced the game to this south western town. They created a sufficient enough test of golf to attract the Irish Professional Championship nearly 80 years later, in 1973, when J. Kinsella lifted the trophy.

Mature trees and many shrubs frequent the fairways of Limerick, so that a premium is put on accuracy and keeping the ball in play. Length isn't really a big factor over this course. For example, the first is a par-4 of just 300 yards and there are eight other par-4s under 400 yards.

The par-3s will not have you reaching for a long iron or fairway wood either: these measure 174-yards (the 5th), 131-yards (8th) and 154-yards (14th).

The same is true of the three par-5s; and even the longest of the trio only read 512 yards on the card from the back tee. Needless to say they are meat and drink for the big hitters

Birdies can be had on this pleasant parkland course as long as you do what every good golfer is supposed to do – hit the fairways and greens.

The three shot holes are on the front nine, so that par out is 37, while 35 is the par for the incoming holes. All in all the course stretches to just under 6,300 yards to a par of 72. Its length really precludes the course from attracting the top tournaments, but the need for accuracy will provide enough of a challenge to the handicap golfer.

COURSE INFORMATION & FACILITIES

Limerick Golf Club
Bally Clough,
Limerick.

Secretary: Declan McDonogh.
Tel: 061-415146. Fax: 061-415146.

Golf Professional
Tel: 0412492.

Green Fees:
Weekdays – IR£22.50.
No visitors on Tuesdays or at Weekends.

CARD OF THE COURSE (metres) – PAR 72

1	2	3	4	5	6	7	8	9	Out
297	426	419	337	149	456	371	110	438	3003
Par 4	Par 5	Par 4	Par 4	Par 3	Par 5	Par 4	Par 3	Par 5	Par 37

10	11	12	13	14	15	16	17	18	In
379	331	370	270	132	297	287	318	312	2696
Par 4	Par 4	Par 4	Par 4	Par 3	Par 4	Par 4	Par 4	Par 4	Par 35

HOW TO GET THERE

5 miles south of Limerick
ty on R511 to Fedamore.

Limerick
Golf Club

Adare

*T*he village of Adare in County Limerick is just what you would expect of rural Ireland, a picturesque village standing on the banks of a river, the Maigue, with thatched cottages and a few pubs. There is also a stately home here, which was the one time ancestral home of the Earls of Dunraven. Now it's a splendid hotel, with an equally splendid golf course.

Adare Manor Golf Club is the work of Robert Trent Jones, and ranks among the best inland courses in Ireland, even though it was only created in 1995.

What you will remember from your round at Adare is the 18th, the course's signature hole. It's a 544-yard, par-5 which calls for a confident third shot. For some 450 yards, the Maigue runs along the left hand side of the fairway, before it turns right to bisect the fairway before the green.

Two large trees on the right hand side of the fairway force you further left than you would like. From here you need a confident pitch to a green that isn't as large as you've been accustomed to throughout the other 17 holes.

Mature trees are to be found on some holes, while others are quite open. The course itself can be described as a gently rolling parkland with not much elevation, making it a joy to walk. You will find water on about 10 holes, in the shape of the Maigue itself, a small tributary, two ponds and a large lake. Besides the 18th, the greens are large. If you are prone to under clubbing your approach shots, then you may spend the day three putting.

A good, enjoyable course if played from sensible tees. Make sure you're playing well if you decide to play from the back tees, where Adare stretches to some 7,100 yards.

COURSE INFORMATION & FACILITIES

Adare Manor Hotel & Golf Club
Adare,
Co. Limerick.

Golf Administrator: Linda Cross.
Tel: 061-395044. Fax: 061-396987.

Green Fees:
Weekdays – IR£40. Weekends – IR£40.
Weekdays (day) – IR£40. Weekends (day) – IR£40.

CARD OF THE COURSE – PAR 72

1	2	3	4	5	6	7	8	9	Out
433	413	403	180	419	205	537	427	577	3594
Par 4	Par 4	Par 4	Par 3	Par 4	Par 3	Par 5	Par 4	Par 5	Par 36

10	11	12	13	14	15	16	17	18	In
441	187	550	442	425	370	170	415	544	3544
Par 4	Par 3	Par 5	Par 4	Par 4	Par 4	Par 3	Par 4	Par 5	Par 36

HOW TO GET THERE

:ated 20 miles from
annon Airport on the
lee/Killarney Road. The
tel and Golf course are
:ated in the village
Adare.

Adare Manor Hotel & Golf Club

Adare Manor, a RAC 5 Star Hotel with sixty-four luxury bedrooms is located only 20 miles from Shannon Airport. The Manor offers the finest of Irish Hospitality.

Within the 840 acre estate of Adare Manor, the indoor facilities include a heated swimming pool, fitness centre, sauna and massage therapy. Outdoor activities include horseriding, clay pigeon shooting and fishing and golf on a championship designed course.

ADARE MANOR HOTEL & GOLF CLUB
ADARE, CO LIMERICK, IRELAND

Telephone Adare Manor 061 396566. Telephone Adare Golf Club 061 395044
Facsimile: 061 396124/396987   USA Toll Free Reservations 800 462 3273

Ballybunion

The global popularity of Ballybunion can be pinpointed to Tom Watson, five times winner of the Open Championship. Watson fell in love with Ballybunion the first time he played it. So much so that he began to prepare for the Open Championship by spending the week before at Ballybunion. Watson's five Open victories proves that Ballybunion is a good test of golf.

There is no doubt the Old Course at Ballybunion is one of the best links courses in the world. You get the sense that this is going to be special when you stand on the first tee. To the right, within driving distance, is a cemetery. No doubt it is full of the lost souls who failed at Ballybunion.

Keep clear of the cemetery and the first is relatively easy, but the second gives a sampling of what's to come. This is a man-size par-4, with a second shot played to an elevated green. Make par here and you'll be on your way to a good round.

The fourth and fifth holes, two relatively plain par-5s, are the only two really weak holes on the course. After that Ballybunion Old becomes a joy and a challenge. Most notable holes include the 6th, 7th and 8th, the 11th, 15th, 16th and 17th. Beauties all that would grace any links.

There is a second course at Ballybunion, the Cashen Course. It's a Robert Trent Jones layout that has caused much controversy since it was built in 1984. Some love it, some hate it. Taken in isolation it's actually a testing links. Narrow fairways and elevated greens are the order of the day on this layout. If you are at Ballybunion, you might as well play it. Then at least you'll know what all the fuss is about.

COURSE INFORMATION & FACILITIES

Ballybunion Golf Club
Sandhill Road,
Ballybunion, Co. Kerry.

Secretary/Manager: Jim McKenna.
Tel: 068-27146. Fax: 068-27387.

Golf Professional Tel: 068-27146.

Green Fees:
Weekdays – IR£45. Weekends – IR£45.
Weekdays (day) – IR£45. Weekends (day) – IR£45.

CARD OF THE COURSE – PAR 71

1	2	3	4	5	6	7	8	9	Out
392	445	220	520	524	364	432	153	454	3495
Par 4	Par 4	Par 3	Par 5	Par 5	Par 4	Par 4	Par 3	Par 4	Par 36

10	11	12	13	14	15	16	17	18	In
359	453	192	484	131	216	499	385	379	3098
Par 4	Par 4	Par 3	Par 5	Par 3	Par 3	Par 5	Par 4	Par 4	Par 35

HOW TO GET THERE

om Shannon Airport, take
ast road N69 to Ballybunion.
mile through town to Club
ouse.

Tralee

If you've seen the movie Ryan's Daughter, then you probably know that Tralee possesses one of the world's most glorious beaches, not to mention scenery that is unrivalled anywhere in Ireland.

The scenery hits you from the moment you get to the first green and second tee. The vista is simply breathtaking, and it's something you will have to put up with for the rest of the round. Oh well, these things are meant to try us, aren't they.

Arnold Palmer and Ed Seay are responsible for the layout at Tralee. Palmer had always wanted to create an Irish course and was given the opportunity in the early 1980s.

Like the scenery, there are some holes at Tralee that will take your breath away. The second, for example, is a par-5 that tracks along cliffs with a green at the very edge of the cliff. Hit the ball off-line and it will land on the rocks far below.

The 3rd hole is reminiscent of the 7th at Pebble Beach, calling for a shot to be played to a green where the Atlantic Ocean is very much in play.

On the back nine you will no doubt find the par-4, 12th hole one of the most demanding two shotters in all of golf. At 434-yards, it calls for a good drive and then an extremely testing approach shot that must be played over a ravine to a plateau green. Make four here and you will feel like you've birdied the hole. You must also play a shot over a deep chasm to find the putting surface of the 13th. Thankfully it's only a 150-yard, par-3. The bad news is that there are days when you will need to hit a wood into the wind.

Don't worry if you play poorly at Tralee, just enjoy the scenery.

HOW TO GET THERE

om Tralee, take the road to
dfert. After 11 km, take the
t turn to Spa/Fenit. After
km, take the right turn to
rrow Harbour and after the
idge take the left fork.

COURSE INFORMATION & FACILITIES

Tralee Golf Club
West Barrow, Ardfert, Tralee,
Co. Kerry.

Club Supervisor: Michael O'Brien.
Tel: 066-36379. Fax: 066-36008.

Green Fees per 18 holes:
Weekdays – IR£30 pre-booked. IR£45 on the day.
Weekends – IR£40 (one round only).
Weekdays (day) – £60. Restrictions apply.

CARD OF THE COURSE (metres) – PAR 71

1	2	3	4	5	6	7	8	9	Out
368	542	183	388	391	389	143	354	451	3209
Par 4	Par 5	Par 3	Par 4	Par 4	Par 4	Par 3	Par 4	Par 5	Par 36

10	11	12	13	14	15	16	17	18	In
385	530	417	145	367	273	181	323	422	3043
Par 4	Par 5	Par 4	Par 3	Par 4	Par 4	Par 3	Par 4	Par 4	Par 35

Killarney

The town of Killarney is a natural starting point for visiting the famous Ring of Kerry and its spectacular scenery – the only problem is, once in Killarney you may never want to leave.

It's a town like no other in Ireland, one with a distinctly cosmopolitan feel. It's also overshadowed by the magnificent Magilicuddy Reeks, the highest mountain range in the Emerald Isle. Golfers are provided with the best view of these magnificent mountains, for only an enchanting lake, Lough Leane, separates Killarney Golf and Fishing Club's two courses from the Reeks.

The two courses are named Mahony's Point and Killeen, with the latter being the longer and more challenging. Indeed the Killeen course hosted the 1991 and 1992 Irish Opens, won both times by Nick Faldo.

While Mahony's Point takes a back seat to the Killeen course when it comes to staging big tournaments, don't think it's not worth

playing – it is. Just to play the last three holes is worth the green fee alone. The trio involves flirting with the water of Lough Leane – for the approach shot to the par-5 16th, and for the entire length of 17 and 18. The 18th, especially, will stick in your memory. Henry Longhurst once described it as the best short hole in the world. No wonder, it calls for a long iron or wood over the lake to find the putting surface.

Killeen also makes good use of the lake on some holes, especially at the first, third, fourth and fifth holes. However, the best hole on the course, and maybe of the entire complex, is the 13th, a long par-4 calling for an accurate second to be played over a stream set down in a little hollow to a long green that falls away to the left. Par here is a good score. But don't be too worried about your score the first time you play Killarney.

Enjoy the scenery, smell the flowers and pack your camera. You'll be enchanted.

COURSE INFORMATION & FACILITIES

Killarney Golf & Fishing Club
(Mahony's Point), Killarney,
Co. Kerry.

Secretary: Tom Prendergast.
Tel: 064-31034. Fax: 064-33065.

Golf Professional
Tel: 064-31615. Fax: 064-33065.

Green Fees:
Weekdays – IR£35.00. Weekends – IR£35.00.
Handicap Certificate required

CARD OF THE COURSE – PAR 72

1	2	3	4	5	6	7	8	9	Out
341	404	431	141	448	360	169	532	296	3122
Par 4	Par 4	Par 4	Par 3	Par 5	Par 4	Par 3	Par 5	Par 4	Par 36

10	11	12	13	14	15	16	17	18	In
344	426	216	435	364	268	458	373	179	3042
Par 4	Par 4	Par 3	Par 5	Par 4	Par 4	Par 5	Par 4	Par 3	Par 36

HOW TO GET THERE

:ilometres west of Killarney
wn – on Ring of Kerry Road.
62 to Killorglin.

HOTEL EUROPE
KILLARNEY'S MOST LUXURIOUS HOTEL

Surrounded by spectacular countryside, the Five Star Hotel Europe is situated overlooking the famous Lakes of Killarney. You will be captivated by its luxurious decor and friendly atmosphere. Each area is furnished with care, right down to the last detail. Our facilities include 25m indoor swimming pool, sauna and gymnasium, free horseriding, free indoor tennis, billiards, fishing and boating on the Lakes of Killarney. Within easy reach of all major Golf Courses. The hotel's conference and meeting facilities are state-of-the-art and include a 450 seat auditorium with built-in microphones and interpreter system. We can also offer two more conference centres with several syndicate rooms. You will enjoy our friendly atmosphere at Hotel Europe.

Hotel Europe, Killarney, Co. Kerry. Tel: 064-31900, Fax: 064-32118
Email: khl@iol.ie, Webb Page: http://www.iol.ie/khl

Dooks

*I*t's very easy to by-pass Dooks Golf Club – not advisable, but very easy. Most golfers hurry past this fine little links course on their way to the mightier challenge of Waterville.

Thankfully enough golfers have slowed down and actually stopped to have a look at the Dooks course. Those who have returned to play have spread the word that this is a little gem of an 18-holer.

It wasn't always 18 holes, though. Founded in 1889, Dooks was a nine hole course until 1970, when the members decided to do something about it. This was in the days long before EEC money was available to upgrade Irish leisure facilities. Having little money with which to pay for the expansion, the club took a pragmatic approach. A committee of nine was formed and each

was responsible for designing one hole!

For less than £3,000, the task was finished with the holes built by the members themselves. The result is terrific. True, Dooks wouldn't test the greatest golfers in the game not at just 6,000 yards. However, it's as much fun as you're likely to find anywhere.

Here you find a golf course that has the feel of a traditional links, one where you will find it hard to spot the new holes from the old (the new are the 4th through the 12th).

Undulating greens that are often raised put a premium on a good short game, so work on your chipping and putting beforehand.

Fine views over Dingle Bay and the mountains of Kerry are to be had here. Try to play it when the sun is setting – it's an enchanting experience.

COURSE INFORMATION & FACILITIES

Dooks Golf Club
Glenbeigh,
Co. Kerry.

Secretary/Manager: Michael Shanahan.
Tel: 066-68205. Fax: 066-68476.

Green Fees:
Weekdays – IR£20. Weekends – IR£20.
Weekdays (day) – IR£28. Weekends (day) – IR£28.

CARD OF THE COURSE – PAR 70

1	2	3	4	5	6	7	8	9	Out
419	131	300	344	194	394	477	368	183	2810
Par 4	Par 3	Par 4	Par 4	Par 3	Par 4	Par 5	Par 4	Par 3	Par 34

10	11	12	13	14	15	16	17	18	In
406	531	370	150	375	213	348	313	494	3200
Par 4	Par 5	Par 4	Par 3	Par 4	Par 3	Par 4	Par 4	Par 5	Par 36

HOW TO GET THERE

...ated on N70 – between
...orglin and Glenbeigh.
...n right at Canagh Bridge
...d continue for 1 mile.

Hotel

Ard na Sidhe

A dream hotel, this romantic Victorian former country house is ideal for all your golfing requirements. Located beside Caragh Lake, this elegant hotel is just 17 miles from Killarney, where the golf courses are considered to be the pick of the Ring of Kerry courses. Once you have mastered the Killarney courses, the area boasts many more of Ireland's most beautiful golf courses for you to conquer.

The hotel awaits you with its homely charm at the end of a tiring day. Built in 1880 by an English lady, who called it the "House of the Fairies", Hotel Ard na Sidhe still resembles a private residence, with valuable antiques, an open fireplace and a magnificent garden. The hotel has twice won first prize in the National Gardens Competition. You can relax, read, go for walks, paint, dream, or simply enjoy yourself in this idyllic setting.

CARAGH LAKE, KILLARNEY, CO. KERRY
Tel: 066/69105 Fax: 066/69282

Beaufort

They often say the place to find a doctor when he's not in his surgery is on the golf course. Well you'll not only find Dr Arthur Spring on the course, but probably building it as well.

A very fine amateur player, Spring packed away his medicine books after 20 years and decided it was time he started designing golf courses. He's done about seven courses in Ireland, and Beaufort is one of them.

Just five miles from Killarney, this par-71 layout was opened in 1995 and offers some great views of the famous MacGillicuddy Reeks. This is as pure a parkland course as you're going to get, with few trees, not much water and very easy walking.

While the course appears fairly wide open, it can be deceptive. Deep rough can leave you just playing back to the fairway, while the creatively contoured greens will put a premium on your short game. Dr Spring had help in this department, in the shape of Tommy Sheerin. Sheerin worked with the one and only Jack Nicklaus on the creation of Mount Juliet, so he knew a thing or three about building greens with subtle contours.

Beaufort lies on the Churchtown Estate, which is dominated by a Georgian manor house built in 1740 by Sir Rolan Blennerhassett.

Beaufort contains many fine holes, but two short par-4s stand out. The green of the 336-yard, 10th makes this hole special, given that the contours resemble three leaves. Putting here can be an adventure. The dogle right, 369-yard, 5th only calls for a pitching wedge or 9-iron, but it must be accurately played to a well bunkered, elevated green.

Dr Spring was wise to change careers.

COURSE INFORMATION & FACILITIES

Beaufort Golf Course
Churchtown, Beaufort,
Killarney, Co. Kerry.

Secretary: Colm Kelly.
Tel: 064-44440. Fax: 064-44752.

Green Fees:
Weekdays – IR£25. Weekends – IR£30.
Weekdays (day) – IR£35. Weekends (day) – IR£42.
Some time restrictions.

CARD OF THE COURSE – PAR 71

1	2	3	4	5	6	7	8	9	Out
504	191	435	356	342	454	383	187	511	3363
Par 5	Par 3	Par 4	Par 4	Par 4	Par 4	Par 4	Par 3	Par 5	Par 36

10	11	12	13	14	15	16	17	18	In
314	428	486	198	400	381	424	195	416	3242
Par 4	Par 4	Par 5	Par 3	Par 4	Par 4	Par 4	Par 3	Par 4	Par 35

HOW TO GET THERE

e N72 west of Killarney
6 miles. Turn off left for
aufort Village. Take first
it in the village - 2 miles
Golf Club.

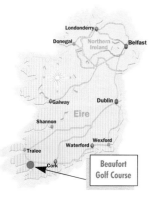

— HOTEL —
DUNLOE CASTLE
KILLARNEY, CO. KERRY

Hotel Dunloe Castle is situated in the midst of a fascinating park landscape. The Green Isle's magic is reflected in the hotel park, a botanic collection of international renown which has won several awards. An unbelievable assortment of flowers and plants flourishes here, and there are Haflinger horses grazing. Everything smells fresh, the world appears to stand still. The castle ruins are reminiscent of the past. From the park you can look out towards the famous Gap of Dunloe, where you can take in the beauties of unspoilt nature The hotel's furnishings are elegant and comfortable. Its stylish decor and numerous exquisite details convey a magnificent sense of atmosphere. Excellent cuisine awaits you in the restaurant.

Telephone: 064/44111   Fax: 064/44583

Waterville

Jack Mulcahy was an Irish born American who, after making millions in the chemical business, sought a reason to return to Ireland for good. That reason became a golf course on the remote west coast of Ireland at Waterville.

Eddie Hackett was the man Mulcahy entrusted to create one of the finest links in all of golf. Built in 1973, it didn't take long for Waterville's reputation to grow. Now it's on the itinerary of every visiting American golfer.

Waterville is just about as natural a links course as you will find anywhere. True it starts slowly with the first and second being slightly inland, but by the time you get to the 417 yard, par 4, 3rd hole you know you're in for a treat. This hole is a slicer's nightmare, for the entire right hand side of the fairway hugs the Atlantic Ocean.

It is on the back nine that Waterville lives up to its premier billing. That's when you get to the meat of the course, so to speak. The 11th and 12th for example, are links holes that would grace any great seaside course. Eleven is a 496 yard, par 5 called Tranquillity which is played over a roller-coaster fairway through an avenue of tall dunes. It is one of the best par 5s in golf.

The 12th is called the Mass hole because priests used to say Mass in a large hollow immediately below the green during a time in Irish history when Catholicism was outlawed. You won't find priests today, but you may just pray that your ball reaches the plateau green.

Best view of the course is provided by Mulcahy's Peak, which is the teeing area for the superb par 3, 17th. Sit here for as long as you possibly can without holding up the group behind. The views are stunning. So is Waterville

COURSE INFORMATION & FACILITIES

Waterville Golf Links
Waterville,
Co. Kerry.

Manager: Noel Cronin.
Tel: 066-74102. Fax: 066-74482.

Golf Professional Tel: 066-74102.

Green Fees:
Weekdays – IR£45. Weekends – IR£45.
Handicap certificates required.

CARD OF THE COURSE – PAR 72

1	2	3	4	5	6	7	8	9	Out
430	469	417	179	595	371	178	435	445	3519
Par 4	Par 4	Par 4	Par 3	Par 5	Par 4	Par 3	Par 4	Par 4	Par 35

10	11	12	13	14	15	16	17	18	In
475	496	200	518	456	392	350	196	582	3665
Par 4	Par 5	Par 3	Par 5	Par 4	Par 4	Par 4	Par 3	Par 5	Par 37

HOW TO GET THERE

ated half way on the Ring
erry. ¹/₄ mile off the main
off Kerry Road, on the
t.

Waterville
Golf Club

Waterville House & Golf Links

Encounter a Mystical Links . . .
Golf in the Kingdom of Kerry

Waterville House is a four star, 18th century manor house. The property features the natural beauty of a forty acre estate on the Atlantic, and most famous sea trout and salmon fishery in Ireland. Aside from its comfort and charm, Waterville House has ten bedrooms en-suite, sauna, steam room, billiard room, outdoor heated pool and private golf practice facility. Guests of Waterville House enjoy preferential tee times, green fees and access to fishing in private lakes and rivers.

Golf at Waterville is a mystical experience – the beauty of classic links land, surrounded by the sea, yet forever challenged and shaped by the elements. Over 100 years old, Waterville is rated among the top 5 courses in Ireland and the top 20 links in the world. The clubhouse is all-inclusive, with locker facilities, proshop and adjacent golf school. An extensive collection of old photographs, golf art and memorabilia enhance the ambiance created by the mixture of visitors with the local membership. The restaurant and bar feature fresh sea food, Irish fare and the best pint in Kerry, all served by the glow of turf fires.

WATERVILLE, CO. KERRY, IRELAND
Tel: 353 66 74244 Fax: 353 66 74567
Village of Waterville located on the Ring of Kerry between Lough Currane and the Atlantic Ocean

Lee Valley

*C*hristy O'Connor Jnr is making something of a name for himself as a golf course architect, and his creation at Lee Valley at Clashanure, Ovens, some five miles from the city of Cork, only adds to his growing reputation.

If you feel something mysterious in the air at Lee Valley, it is probably because of the presence of an ancient ring fort. It is said that the legendary Irish giant Finn McCool – the one responsible for the odd rock formations on the Causeway Coast near Royal Portrush – once threw a stone over 4 miles from this fort.

The fort stand near Lee Valley's 12th, 13th and 14th holes, so watch out because ancient spirits may be at work around these holes. Modern spirits are also in play on this layout, in the shape of water hazards, which come into play on a number of holes.

Lee Valley has the best of the old and modern worlds, for besides an ancient for the course also has a superb floodlit driving range together with a well equipped clubhouse.

O'Connor may have been thinking of the first at Portstewart when he designed the first at Lee Valley. Like the magnificent links hole on Portstewart, Lee Valley's opener is a downhill dogleg that offers tremendous views of the surrounding countryside.

Christy has set a demanding test at Lee Valley. Besides the water hazards, which are very evident at holes like the 8th and 15th, both par-5s, and the 17th, there are some long, testing holes. However, there is also a good variety of different length holes so that the course is not an out and out slog. It's a layout that will only get better as it matures.

HOW TO GET THERE

ke the N22 from Cork
ward Macroom/Killarney.

e Valley Golf
Country Club

COURSE INFORMATION & FACILITIES

 Lee Valley Golf and Country Club
Clashanure, Ovens,
Co. Cork.

Manager: Kathleen Curron
Tel: 021-331721. Fax: 021-331695.

Golf Professional Tel: 021-331721.

Green Fees:
Weekdays – IR£22.50. Weekends – IR£25.
Weekdays (day) – IR£32.50. Weekends (day) – IR£35.
Restrictions apply.

CARD OF THE COURSE – PAR ?

1	2	3	4	5	6	7	8	9	Out
345	331	165	504	457	153	436	511	303	3205
Par 4	Par 4	Par 3	Par 5	Par 4	Par 3	Par 4	Par 5	Par 4	Par 36

10	11	12	13	14	15	16	17	18	In
314	522	166	358	389	525	160	394	381	3229
Par 4	Par 5	Par 3	Par 4	Par 4	Par 5	Par 3	Par 4	Par 4	Par 36

Old Head

There have been many new courses built in Ireland in the past 10 years, and many that can be considered true championship links. However, the most spectacular of the new breed is the Old Head Golf Links at Kinsale.

The Old Head has been laid out on a rocky promontory that juts out into the sea. You drive into the course through a narrow spit of land that opens out into what was formerly just poor farmland and a haven for birds. On all sides the land drops dramatically down to the sea, where the water crashes onto the dark rocks. The cliff edges have been fully incorporated into the design of the holes, so that no less than nine play along the very edge of the promontory.

There is no room for error on the holes along the edge of the Old Head. Even if you are a touch wayward you can find yourself reaching for another ball. There is just no safety area if you fire at some flags, for your ball will disappear into the depths of the sea. Best among the holes hard by the sea is the 16th. Here you play from a high tee to a green that is literally one step from a long drop to the rocks below. Push or slice the ball and you will be in trouble, deep trouble.

Even off the tee on some of the cliff holes you can find yourself reloading. The 12th, for example, is a dramatic par-5 that asks you to hit across fresh air towards an elusive fairway. A bird sanctuary is located on the cliff face to your left. Concentration can be just a trifle tough.

You have to play this course at least once. You won't find a course as dramatic anywhere else in Ireland.

COURSE INFORMATION & FACILITIES

Old Head Golf Links
Kinsale,
Co. Cork.

Membership/Events Executive: Fiona MacDonald.
Tel: 021-778444.

Golf Professional:
Tel: 021-778444.

Green Fees:
Weekdays – IR£50. Weekends – IR£50.
Weekdays (Day) – IR£80.
Weekends (Day) – IR£80.

CARD OF THE COURSE – PAR 72

1	2	3	4	5	6	7	8	9	Out
420	387	153	407	405	488	164	496	449	3369
Par 4	Par 4	Par 3	Par 3	Par 4	Par 4	Par 5	Par 3	Par 4	Par 36

10	11	12	13	14	15	16	17	18	In
493	180	498	222	429	340	186	628	411	3387
Par 5	Par 3	Par 5	Par 3	Par 4	Par 4	Par 3	Par 5	Par 4	Par 36

HOW TO GET THERE

in Road from Cork to
sale (R600). Through
sale Town and take the
d to Sarretstown/Old Head
Kinsale (R606).

Cork

Any fan of Dr Alister MacKenzie will want to pay a visit to Cork Golf Club at Little Island, for the creator of Augusta National is partly responsible for this course.

Cork Golf Club was formed in 1888 on a different piece of land to which the present 18 hole course occupies today. In 1898 the club moved to its present location beside the Lee Estuary where nine holes were laid out by Tom Dunn, the club's first professional. Thirty years later the club expanded to 18 holes and MacKenzie was called in to add the new nine and revise the existing holes.

Further changes were made to the course in 1975, when Frank Pennink was called in to make revisions.

Cork has been considered good enough to have hosted many important tournaments, including the 1932 Irish Open, the 1940 Irish Professional Championship and the Carrolls International in 1965. As well as these professional events, the club has been venue for many of the country's top amateur tournaments.

What these players faced at Cork are MacKenzie's trade mark - large, undulating greens. Indeed, play Cork without three putting and you can count yourself a good putter.

A limestone quarry has been incorporated into the golf course, and comes into play from the 6th hole, which calls for a short pitch shot to a green where the walls of the old quarry are very much in play.

The Lee Estuary also comes into play at Cork, especially at the par-4, 4th hole. This is a great two shotter which calls for your drive to cut off as much of the estuary as possible to allow you to reach the green in two at this 450-yard hole.

The closing holes are not quite as dramatic as those that come beforehand, but they are played in the most pleasant of parkland surroundings.

COURSE INFORMATION & FACILITIES

Cork Golf Club
Little Island,
Co. Cork.

General Manager: Matt Sands.
Tel: 021-353451. Fax: 021-353410.

Golf Professional: 021-353421.

Green Fees:
Weekdays – IR£33. Weekends – IR£38.
Weekdays (day) – IR£33.
Letter of introduction required.

CARD OF THE COURSE (metres) – PAR 72

1	2	3	4	5	6	7	8	9	Out
340	460	244	411	510	300	169	379	178	2991
Par 4	Par 5	Par 4	Par 4	Par 5	Par 4	Par 3	Par 4	Par 3	Par 36

10	11	12	13	14	15	16	17	18	In
374	454	289	157	397	383	323	360	387	3124
Par 4	Par 5	Par 4	Par 3	Par 4	Par 4	Par 4	Par 4	Par 4	Par 36

HOW TO GET THERE

miles east of Cork city, off
5 road.

Fota Island

*T*ake one of Britain's top amateurs and one of Ireland best professionals, ask them to create their idea of a great golf course and what do you get? Fota Island, that's what.

Two time British Amateur Champion (1977-78) Peter McEvoy – the last British Amateur Champion to make the cut at The Masters incidentally – and four time European Tour winner Christy O'Connor Jnr are responsible for Fota Island, which lies about 15 minutes drive from Cork.

The golf course is one of the prettiest you will find in all of Ireland. It is situated next door to the Fota Island Arboretum and Gardens, so if you've got a green thumb you'll be well pleased.

Obviously McEvoy and O'Connor know a few things about good golf course design, and they've brought that knowledge to Fota Island. This is a par-72 course that runs to

nearly 6,900 yards, one that will require you to use every club in the bag. Indeed, if you play from the back tees you may find yourself staring down long iron second shots on a number of par-4s. There are no fewer than seven par-4s that measure 417-yards or longer.

Three of those long par-4s are to be found on the run-in, as 14, 15 and 16 measure 440, 455 and 417-yards respectively. Seventeen isn't much of breather either – it plays to 209-yards!

McEvoy obviously learnt from his two visits to Augusta National to play in The Masters, for Fota's greens are quite undulating. However, they are built to the highest standard so that every putt rolls true.

Water comes into play quite a lot at Fota Island, so take lots of balls if you're a bit wayward.

COURSE INFORMATION & FACILITIES

 Fota Island Golf Club
Carrigtwohill,
Co. Cork.

General Manager: Kevin Mulcaly.
Tel: 021-883700. Fax: 021-883713.

Golf Professional Tel: 021-883710.

Green Fees:
Weekdays – IR£28. Weekends – IR£23.
Weekdays (day) – IR£40. Weekends (day) – IR£48.

CARD OF THE COURSE – PAR 72

1	2	3	4	5	6	7	8	9	Out
428	435	182	501	577	375	170	484	425	3577
Par 4	Par 4	Par 3	Par 5	Par 5	Par 4	Par 3	Par 5	Par 4	Par 37

10	11	12	13	14	15	16	17	18	In
502	201	425	183	440	455	417	209	492	3324
Par 5	Par 3	Par 4	Par 3	Par 4	Par 4	Par 4	Par 3	Par 5	Par 35

HOW TO GET THERE

ke N25 east from Cork city
vards Waterford and
sslare. After about 9 miles
it for Fota Island/Cobh.
trance is 1500m
m N25 exit on
ht.

South East

The South East

*A*s Killarney is to County Kerry and the Southwest of Ireland, Kinsale is to the Southeast corner of this beautiful island. Indeed, Kinsale is often referred to as the gourmet capital of Ireland. Eat in some of it' fine restaurants and you'll know why. In times past, Kinsale wasn't always a premier attraction for golfers. However, now there's a perfect reason to travel there. The lure is a course by the name of the Old Head Golf Links, a stunning new course that sits on a rocky promontory that juts out into the sea. Here you will find no less than nine holes with the tee or the green, sometimes both, hanging on the edge of a cliff, with the sea crashing on the rocks far below. Hit a few wayward shots here and you will soon waste your supply of golf balls. This corner of Ireland is also famous for cut glass, for it is in this region that you will find Waterford. You will also find a few courses not far from the crystal factory that are well worth a visit. Until 1991 there was really only two courses to speak of in this area – Tramore and Waterford Golf Club. Mind you, they were courses you could speak volumes about. Waterford, for example, was designed by Willie Park and with later alterations by James Braid. Whenever two Open champions have a hand in the creation of any course, it is well worth playing. In recent times the number of Irish courses has simply mushroomed. European money was responsible for this explosion, and many clubs have come into being throughout the island. The boom in Irish golf has not missed Waterford. There are at least four courses in the area that have been developed from 1991. (Who knows, by the time you read this there may be a few more). Dunmore East, Faithlegg, Waterford Castle and West Waterford have all come into existence in the '90s, making the region an attractive destination for visiting golfers. Waterford Castle is especially worthy of a visit. A Des Smyth designed layout, the golf course sits on an island in the River Suir. Don't worry if the odd boat passes you by, it'll only add to your round of golf. This region not one frequented by many visiting golfers, so you

may find it easier to get a game than areas such as Dublin, Kerry and Northern Ireland. Although with the number of good new courses, it's a safe bet that this area will soon be attracting more and more golfers. The fact that it's only a short drive from Cork Airport is also a bonus. Depending on where you live, you could be just two hours from your front door to a game of golf.

COUNTY TIPPERARY
WEST WATERFORD
TRAMORE
WATERFORD CASTLE

FAITHLEGG
ST. HELEN'S BAY
MOUNT JULIET

County Tipperary

The County Tipperary Golf Club and Country Club lies just six miles to the west of Cashel and its famous Rock. Situated on the banks of the River Multeen in the heart of an area known as the Golden Vale, European Tour Professional Philip Walton has created a testing par 72 layout.

The course is set over 150 acres of parkland with mature woodland and many water hazards, including parts of the Multeen which must be negotiated. It stretches to just over 6,700 yards off the back tees with a good variety of holes.

Walton has done well to fashion the course so that it compliments the landscape. Although there are already mature trees on the layout, thousands of new trees have been planted since the course was opened.

Among Walton's favourite holes are the 4th, 12th and 18th, a par-5, 3 and 4 respectively. The 4th is the longest hole on the course at 584 yards, a genuine three shotter with trees on either side off the tee, and the Multeen dissecting the fairway about 100 yards from the green.

Longest of the par-3s is the 195-yard, 12th hole, calling for a long iron to be played to a green guarded by four large bunkers. Walton says a par here is a bonus every time.

The Irish professional particularly likes the finish he has created. The 18th is a par-4 measuring just over 400-yards that doglegs from right to left, with large trees coming into play on the drive. An approach shot over the river to an elusive green makes this an excellent finishing hole.

COURSE INFORMATION & FACILITIES

Co. Tipperary Golf & Country Club
Dundrum House Hotek, Dundrum,
Co. Tipperary.

Director of Golf: William Crowe.
Tel: 062-71116. Fax: 062-71366.

Green Fees:
Weekdays – £18. Weekends – £22.

CARD OF THE COURSE – PAR 72

1	2	3	4	5	6	7	8	9	Out
432	510	168	584	342	366	357	378	470	3607
Par 4	Par 5	Par 3	Par 5	Par 4	Par 4	Par 4	Par 4	Par 4	Par 37

10	11	12	13	14	15	16	17	18	In
385	372	195	360	321	178	508	339	444	3102
Par 4	Par 4	Par 3	Par 4	Par 4	Par 3	Par 5	Par 4	Par 4	Par 35

HOW TO GET THERE

miles west of Cashel Town
on the Cork/Dublin Road –
7, N8.

Dundrum House Hotel

A country manor house of style and warmth reflecting the grace and elegance the house enjoyed in the 18th century. Open log fires greet guests on chilly spring and autumn evenings and the bar, with its beautiful stained glass windows, is the perfect meeting place for guests, golfers and fishermen. Each bedroom and suite enjoys the Georgian generosity of space and comfort as well as the modern additions of a direct dial telephone, TV, central heating and en suite bathroom and toilet. The old world atmosphere and hospitality is palpable in the dining room, where fine linen clad tables receive the finest cuisine and wines. Whether your party is small or large, Dundrum House provides the perfect ambience for a perfect meal.

DUNDRUM/CASHEL, CO. TIPPERARY, IRELAND
Tel: +353 (0)62 71116   Fax: +353 (0)62 71366

West Waterford

*T*om and Nora Spratt are the proud owners of the course called West Waterford at Coolcormack near Dungarvan. Tom and Nora sacrificed 150 acres of their farm to create the golf course. Thankfully they had the good sense not to try a do-it-yourself job. They decided to call in an expert, and they got the best in Irish golf – Eddie Hackett.

Hackett doesn't fool around when it comes to golf course design, as anyone will contest who's played the numerous other Irish courses he's designed. True to form, you will find West Waterford a fairly man-sized golf course.

Hackett has done a good job with the land made available to him. He gets top marks for the way he's incorporated the beautiful River Brickey into the layout,

especially on the back nine where it comes into play more than most golfers would like.

West Waterford is the type of golf course you can score well on, for there are a lot of holes in the 300-yard bracket. For example, the course features six par-4s that range from 336 yards to 397 yards.

You will find the back nine slightly tougher than the outward half. For one the river comes into play, and two the last three holes combined measure over 1,500 yards. The final trio consists of a 523-yard, par-5; a 424-yard, par-4; and a 575-yard par-5. In other words, try to make your score before the final three, as they can be potential card wreckers.

Overall the course stretches to just over 6,800 yards and plays to a par of 72. Many of the holes provide good views of the Comeragh and Knockmealdown mountains.

COURSE INFORMATION & FACILITIES

West Waterford Golf Club
Dungarvan,
Co. Waterford.

Secretary: Austin A. Spratt.
Tel: 00353-58-43216. Fax: 00353-58-44343.

Green Fees:
Weekdays – IR£17. Weekends – IR£22.
Booking essential.

CARD OF THE COURSE – PAR 72

1	2	3	4	5	6	7	8	9	Out
511	357	381	191	487	404	383	361	233	3308
Par 5	Par 4	Par 4	Par 3	Par 5	Par 4	Par 4	Par 4	Par 3	Par 36
10	11	12	13	14	15	16	17	18	In
431	173	459	169	407	333	523	424	576	3494
Par 4	Par 3	Par 4	Par 3	Par 4	Par 4	Par 5	Par 4	Par 5	Par 36

HOW TO GET THERE

:m west of Dungarvan off
25 by-pass on Aglish Road.

est Waterford
Golf Club

Tramore

Tramore Golf Club started out as a seaside course away back in 1894. However, the members have been gradually forced inland over the years.

Flooding from the sea forced the first move. Sea water broke through protective sand banks surrounding the original 9-hole layout, flooding the course. As a temporary measure, a new course was created inside the local racetrack until, in 1939, Tramore occupied the present site. The new location allowed the club to expand to the 18 holes which exist today.

Tramore was honoured in 1987 when the Irish Close Championship was held there. Eddie Power won the event that year, but being a member of the club he had the benefit of local knowledge. While the increased length of today's professionals might make it a bit short for the game's top players, at 6,700 yards Tramore is worthy of the game's top amateurs. Besides the Irish Close, the Irish Ladies Amateur Championship has been held there twice, in 1975 and '88. It's also a good course that all levels of handicap will enjoy.

Fairly flat with broad fairways and not too many bunkers, Tramore can offer up good scores. Excellent turf and equally excellent putting surfaces mean you should seldom find a poor lie or need to complain about bad greens. It doesn't pay to be too overconfident, though, for there are some tricky doglegs and holes that call for accuracy off the tee.

Many trees were planted when the course was created and now provide definition and a splendid backdrop for many of the holes.

CARD OF THE COURSE (metres) – PAR 72

1	2	3	4	5	6	7	8	9	Out
365	455	155	344	294	159	367	371	506	3016
Par 4	Par 5	Par 3	Par 4	Par 4	Par 3	Par 4	Par 4	Par 5	Par 36

10	11	12	13	14	15	16	17	18	In
174	366	315	366	406	117	500	346	449	3039
Par 3	Par 4	Par 4	Par 4	Par 4	Par 3	Par 5	Par 4	Par 5	Par 36

HOW TO GET THERE

lf a mile from Tramore on
ungarvan Coast Road.

Waterford Castle

Waterford Castle is unique among Irish golf courses as the only way to get to it is via a ferry. The course is situated just a few miles to the east of the famous glass making city on an island in the River Suir estuary. A small ferry for about six cars takes you to the island.

Needless to say, there is also a castle on the island, an imposing edifice that dates back to the 11th century. It once belonged to the Fitzgerald clan, a powerful family in this part of Ireland in years gone by.

Waterford Castle is another creation by Des Smyth, a veteran and seven time winner on the European Tour. Along with Declan Branigan, a former Irish International player who has collaborated with Smyth on other projects, the Irish pro has fashioned a good par-72 course in an idyllic setting.

This is essentially a parkland course that will need time to mature. Only opened in 1992, many trees have been planted and will take some time to grow. However, Waterford Castle is a good test of golf, particularly from the back tees where the course stretches to over 6,800 yards. Here you will find a variety of demanding par-3, 4 and 5 holes.

Waterford Castle is surrounded by good views of the River Suir. An added bonus are the boats that sail along it to get to the port of Waterford.

COURSE INFORMATION & FACILITIES

Waterford Castle Golf Club
The Island, Ballinakill,
Waterford.

Golf Administrator: Ann Dempsey.
Tel: 051-871633. Fax: 051-871634.

Green Fees:
Weekdays – IR£22. Weekends – IR£25.
Weekdays (day) – IR£32. Weekends (day) – IR£35.
Time restrictions apply.

CARD OF THE COURSE (metres) – PAR 72

1	2	3	4	5	6	7	8	9	Out
385	176	372	356	476	315	193	452	381	3106
Par 4	Par 3	Par 4	Par 4	Par 5	Par 4	Par 3	Par 5	Par 4	Par 36

10	11	12	13	14	15	16	17	18	In
160	346	415	463	343	468	187	368	353	3103
Par 3	Par 4	Par 4	Par 5	Par 4	Par 5	Par 3	Par 4	Par 4	Par 36

HOW TO GET THERE

5 to Tower Hotel – turn
 to Dunmore, East Road –
prox 2 miles to Waterford
gional Hospital, through
undabout, turn for
aterford Castle
prox 300yds.

Waterford Castle
Golf Club

Granville Hotel

Waterford's prestigious city centre hotel, RAC***, overlooking the river Suir. This family run hotel is one of Ireland's oldest with significant historical connections. It has been elegantly refurbished, retaining its olde world Georgian character. Two award winning restaurants. Bells and Bianconi, bar, en suite bedrooms, board room and conference facilities. Golf, fishing, city and Waterford Crystal tours arranged.

WATERFORD IRELAND
TEL: (051) 855111
FAX: (051) 870307

Faithlegg

If you're going to play Faithlegg, then get lots of putting practice in beforehand. This lovely course in County Waterford is renowned for its undulating greens, placing pressure not only on the short game, but on your approach play as well. Paddy Merrigan is the man responsible for numerous three putts, for he designed Faithlegg.

Merrigan was given a great piece of land on the banks of the River Suir on which to create a golf course that runs to just over 6,700 yards with a par of 72. It's not a conventional 72, however, as the front nine plays to a par of 34, while 38 is the score the scratch man is supposed to match on the inward nine. As you would expect from the above figures, the inward half is much longer than the outward nine, by over 700 yards.

The difference in length of the two nines would seem to indicate that you should take advantage of the outward nine, but that's nc as easy as it sounds. While it's over 700 yard shorter, it's basically because the nine comprises only one par-5 and three par-3s.

The first is fairly short at 293-yards, calling for a drive and a flick. The fourth, too, is no slog at 348-yards, but the other holes aren't easy by any means. There are three par-4s around 400-yards, and the par-3 6th hole measures 205 yards.

The back nine is the complete reverse of the outward half, inasmuch as it contains only one par-3 and three par-5s. Don't expec to tear Faithlegg apart, though, as it's a fairly stiff test for most handicap levels.

Faithlegg is dominated by Faithlegg House, an outstanding building that was buil in 1783. There are plans are to turn the magnificent building into a hotel at some point in the future.

COURSE INFORMATION & FACILITIES

Faithlegg Golf Club
Faithlegg, Cheekpoint,
Co. Waterford.

Director: Ted Higgins.
Tel: 051-382241. Fax: 051-382664.

Green Fees:
Weekdays – IR£22. Weekends –IR£25.
Weekdays (day) – IR£32. Weekends (day) – IR£35.

CARD OF THE COURSE (metres) – PAR 72

1	2	3	4	5	6	7	8	9	Out
268	454	149	319	385	187	378	356	142	2638
Par 4	Par 5	Par 3	Par 4	Par 4	Par 3	Par 4	Par 4	Par 3	Par 34

10	11	12	13	14	15	16	17	18	In
448	362	401	455	465	339	150	395	404	3419
Par 5	Par 4	Par 4	Par 5	Par 5	Par 4	Par 3	Par 4	Par 4	Par 38

OW TO GET THERE

iles from Waterford. Take
more East Road towards
eekpoint village.

the strand inn

Owned and run by the Foyle family for over 30 years. The Strand Inn is ideally situated in a sheltered cove, with an excellent sandy beach and safe swimming within 10 yards.

Our seafood restaurant has a very fine reputation. We take great pride and care with our food. Fish on the menu are landed daily in the harbour opposite. We combine these with crunchy fresh vegetables and herbs, which are grown locally for us. Great steaks and fine wine you won't be disappointed.

With probably the best location in this picturesque village, all our bedrooms are en-suite with TV's and most have balconies overlooking the beach and bay.

2 night specials available.

We have a lovely friendly pub which serves great pints, the perfect place to relax and watch the boats coming and going.

Bar Food served from 12.30 – 2.30pm.

With six golf courses on our doorstep we are the ideal base for the avid golfer. We would be delighted to quote special rates for groups, halfboard or self catering.

Restaurant open from 6.30pm – 10.00pm each evening.

Most credit cards accepted.

dunmore east, co. waterford, ireland
Tel: 051 383174 (Management) 051 383161 (Bars)
Fax: 051 383756

St. Helen's Bay

*M*any Irish courses are steeped in the island's history. On them you will find old castles, or towers or ruined ring forts, all sorts of relics from Ireland's colourful days of yore. Such is St. Helen's Bay.

Situated about three miles from Rosslare Harbour in County Wexford, St. Helens Bay has a 13th century tower near the 12th hole and nearly a mile of stone walls that date back to the Great Potato Famine, a devastating event in Irish history that claimed the lives of about one million people. The walls have been lovingly restored and incorporated into the design of the golf course, for example one of those old walls runs down the right side of the 18th fairway.

St. Helens isn't strictly a links course. Like Seapoint near Dublin, the course is a mixture of parkland and links golf rolled into one. Five lakes have been incorporate into the design, and thousands of trees hav been planted to give definition to some of the holes.

European Tour professional Philip Walton is responsible for the design of St. Helens, and he has created a golf course beside one of the loveliest beaches you will find in all of Ireland. It's called Pirates Cove, for it was used long ago by the bad boys of the seven seas. The last two holes si tight by this beach. Hook the ball at the las and you will be wishing you had thought to bring a bucket and spade, for the ball will b sitting on the sand.

St. Helens measures just under 7,000 from the back tees, but play it from more sensible markers for the wind always blows on this part of the Wexford coastline.

COURSE INFORMATION & FACILITIES

St. Helen's Bay Golf & Country Club
Kilrane, Rosslare Harbour,
Co. Wexford.

Managing Director: Larry Byrne.
Tel: 053-33669/33234. Fax: 053-33803.

Green Fees:
Weekdays – IR£20. Weekends – IR£20. (High)
Weekdays – IR£16. Weekends – IR£20. (Low)

CARD OF THE COURSE (metres) – PAR 72

1	2	3	4	5	6	7	8	9	Out
410	379	192	288	305	308	165	412	478	2937
Par 5	Par 4	Par 3	Par 4	Par 4	Par 4	Par 3	Par 4	Par 5	Par 36

10	11	12	13	14	15	16	17	18	In
488	175	406	419	299	567	368	192	240	3154
Par 5	Par 3	Par 4	Par 4	Par 4	Par 5	Par 4	Par 3	Par 4	Par 36

HOW TO GET THERE

...m Port of Rosslare –
...1 mile at Kilrane and
...ow signs.
...N11 – 90 miles (Dublin)
...t at Kilrane.

Mount Juliet

O f all recent Irish courses laid out on former country estates, Mount Juliet may just be the best. Nick Faldo certainly thinks so – he loves the place.

The main reason Faldo loves the golf course is that it's always in first class condition. The Englishman ostensibly moved to the United States so he could play on good quality courses throughout the year. If European professional tournaments were held on courses like Mount Juliet, he would probably move back home permanently.

Mount Juliet had the best start in life, because the best was brought in to design the golf course. Jack Nicklaus was entrusted with the task of making Mount Juliet the best inland course in Ireland.

Quite simply, Mount Juliet is a top notch course in top notch condition. You won't find better fairways and greens in all of Ireland. You'll be hard pressed to find a better selection of holes too. This a golf course laid out in beautiful parkland, with many ponds and mature trees.

Nicklaus has made excellent use of the land to shape the holes. Best on the front nine is the par-3, 3rd and the par-4, 4th. Th former calls for a good tee shot over water to a green with lots of room on the right bu little on the left. In other words, pray the p is on the right when you get to the tee. The 4th calls for an accurate tee shot to a narro fairway and then an approach to a green with water on the right. Many balls land on the left side of this green.

On the back nine the run of holes from the par-3, 11th to the par-3, 14th is as good stretch as you will find anywhere.

COURSE INFORMATION & FACILITIES

Mount Juliet Golf Club
Thomastown,
Co. Kilkenny.

Golf Manager: Tony Judge.
Tel: 056-24455. Fax: 056-24022.

Golf Professional Tel: 056-24455.

Green Fees:
Weekdays – IR£40. Weekends – IR£50 Winter/Autumn.
Weekdays (day) – IR£65. Weekends (day) – IR£70.

CARD OF THE COURSE – PAR 72

1	2	3	4	5	6	7	8	9	Out
363	414	184	402	534	229	417	577	424	3544
Par 4	Par 4	Par 3	Par 4	Par 5	Par 3	Par 4	Par 5	Par 4	Par 36
10	11	12	13	14	15	16	17	18	In
546	168	417	436	197	371	433	515	474	3557
Par 5	Par 3	Par 4	Par 4	Par 3	Par 4	Par 4	Par 5	Par 4	Par 36

HOW TO GET THERE

m Dublin Airport head
th on M50, then M7 to
AS, M9 to Castledermot
d Carlow – follow main
olin to Waterford
d for 30 minutes
ch leads
mastown.

MOUNT JULIET

ONE OF EUROPE'S GREAT COUNTRY ESTATES

*1,500 walled acres of unspoilt woodland, pasture and
formal gardens, secluded in the southeast of the
country, yet close to Dublin, London and continental cities.*

Enjoy an almost endless variety of outdoor pursuits amid the
magnificent scenery and pure country air of the estate. Mount
Juliet offers a truly unique sporting experience from the most
energetic activities to the more sedate. Built over 200 years ago,
Mount Juliet House still retains an aura of 18th century
grandeur. 32 en-suite bedrooms, each elegantly decorated, retain
their own individual character and ambience.

**Thomastown, County Kilkenny, Ireland
Telephone: 353 56 24455   Fax: 353 56 24522**

Dublin

Dublin

"*In Dublin's fair city where there the girls are so pretty*" is the line to the famous song. Substitute golf courses for girls and you won't get many arguments. Let's face it, if you're going to go to Ireland, then you've got to go to Dublin, haven't you? What could be finer than strolling down O'Connell Street on a sunny day, or standing by the Liffey watching the world go by? The Irish have a term known as the "craic", as in "you'll enjoy the craic." It's a hard term to define, but it basically means enjoying yourself with friends and a few drinks. Nowhere will you experience the craic more than in the capital itself. Dublin has always been a destination for golfers. Portmarnock, Woodbrook and Royal Dublin, all are good enough reason to visit Ireland's capital city. Not surprisingly though, as golf has boomed throughout the island, many of the best new courses are to be found near Dublin. Portmarnock Hotel, Luttrellstown Castle, Druids Glen and The K Club, to name but a few, are all additions to an area already rich in good golf courses. Indeed, you could easily spend a month based in Dublin and never run out of courses to play. First and foremost you have to try to play Portmarnock. It's not easy to get on this fine old links, because it's on everyone's must play list. But if you can beg a round somehow then do so, for it's an experience not to missed. Play it and you soon see why so many Irish Opens have been held there. If you can't get on Portmarnock then fear not, for the Portmarnock Hotel course is reasonable compensation. It was designed by Bernhard Langer and the two time Masters winner has come up with a cracking links course that will suit all levels of golfer. You have to venture out of Dublin to find some of the best courses, with Druid's Glen possibly the best of the new bunch. This is a Pat Ruddy/Tom Craddock designed course that has staged the Irish Open the past couple of years. Europe's finest players find it a tough examination paper. It's a course that calls for straight driving and accurate iron play. Not surprisingly, Colin

Montgomerie has won the title both times it was held there. If you're as straight off the tee as Monty, then you'll have no problem. Otherwise don't expect to match your handicap. Dublin is rich in culture and heritage. It is also rich in fine golf courses. It's yours to explore.

CARLOW
KILKEA CASTLE
RATHSALLAGH
WOODBROOK
DRUIDS GLEN
EUROPEAN

ROYAL DUBLIN
THE K CLUB
LUTTRELLSTOWN
PORTMARNOCK
PORTMARNOCK LINKS

Carlow

arlow is home to the Midland Scratch Cup every October. Such is the quality of this fine inland course that it nearly always attracts a quality field. Among the winners of this prestigious event is Peter McEvoy, who managed to shoot 11 consecutive rounds under 70. That's impressive, given that the course's SSS is 70.

There are only two par-5s on Carlow, the 5th and the 18th, and both offer good birdie opportunities. That's more than can be said about the par-3s, which are elusive birdie holes. Best among these is the 17th, an uphill par-3 which calls for more club than the 152 yards marked on the card. The hole is well bunkered, so an accurate iron shot is need to find the putting surface if you are to have any chance of making a birdie or par.

The 17th is part of a good closing stretch that begins at the tough, 455-yard, par-4, 14th hole. Play well over these holes and you have a chance of returning a good score. The trees, too, seem to encroach on the holes on the back nine, calling for straighter shots on the run in.

Of the holes on the front nine, the 8th is the one that will probably stay in your memory. The tee on this 426-yard, par-4 is the highest point on the course, and the drive must be played downhill through an avenue of tall trees that frame the fairway. A straight drive is a must.

Carlow is blessed with excellent turf, so that golf is virtually playable 12 months of the year.

HOW TO GET THERE

5 miles north of Carlow
wn on the Dublin Road
9).

Carlow
Golf Club

COURSE INFORMATION & FACILITIES

Carlow Golf Club
Deerpark,
Carlow.

Secretary: Margaret Meaney.
Tel: 0503-31695. Fax: 0503-40065.

Golf Professional Tel: 0503-41745.

Green Fees:
Weekdays – IR£20. Weekends – IR£25.

CARD OF THE COURSE (metres) – PAR 70

1	2	3	4	5	6	7	8	9	Out
395	275	124	333	450	163	389	390	335	2857
Par 4	Par 4	Par 3	Par 4	Par 5	Par 3	Par 4	Par 4	Par 4	Par 35

10	11	12	13	14	15	16	17	18	In
273	381	334	150	415	334	393	134	450	2874
Par 4	Par 4	Par 4	Par 3	Par 4	Par 4	Par 4	Par 3	Par 5	Par 35

Kilkea Castle

*A*nother of Ireland's country estates turned into a golf course and hotel, Kilkea Castle is one of the oldest inhabited castles in Ireland, dating back to the 12th century when it was built for Walter de Riddlesford by Hugh de Lacy.

Kilkea Castle sits on the River Greese, and the river serves as a hazard for many of the holes on the accompanying golf course. The 6,700 yard layout was designed by two locals by the name of McDaid and Cassidy, with help from golf professional Andy Gilbert.

Kilkea Castle lies in County Kildare, and its golf course is a strong test from the back markers. Here you will find a host of challenging holes. For example, there are eight par-4s over 400-yards. The par-3s don't quite demand the same sort of length, ranging from 150-yards to 190-yards, but they call for accurate iron shots played to challenging yet receptive greens.

When the river isn't getting in your way, two lakes make sure you don't get respite from water hazards. However, play from sensible tees and this course will suit all handicap levels, from the scratch man to the high handicapper.

Being one of Ireland's oldest, the castle has a lot of history attached to it. Now it is a 45 bedroom hotel where the service and accommodation is top notch. Throw in the excellent leisure facilities and you have a very good golf complex in the heart of County Kildare.

COUNTY KILDARE

HOW TO GET THERE

From the M9, take the N78
to Athy. Turn left after the
Ford garage and continue
for 6 miles.

COURSE INFORMATION & FACILITIES

 Kilkea Castle Hotel & Golf Club
Castledermot,
Co. Kildare.

Secretary/Manager: Adeline Molloy.
Tel: 0503-45156. Fax: 0503-45187.

Green Fees:
Weekdays – IR£25. Weekends – IR£25.
Weekdays (day) – IR£40. Weekends (day) – IR£40.

CARD OF THE COURSE (metres) – PAR 70

1	2	3	4	5	6	7	8	9	Out
365	500	345	170	501	146	387	419	370	3203
Par 4	Par 5	Par 4	Par 3	Par 5	Par 3	Par 4	Par 4	Par 4	Par 36

10	11	12	13	14	15	16	17	18	In
138	383	485	413	170	405	175	337	383	2889
Par 3	Par 4	Par 5	Par 4	Par 3	Par 4	Par 3	Par 4	Par 4	Par 34

119

Rathsallagh

Peter McEvoy and Christy O'Connor Jnr are making a habit of producing good golf courses. They teamed together to create the magnificent Fota Island, and they've done it again with Rathsallagh.

Set in beautiful rolling countryside in County Wicklow some 30 miles from Dublin, Rathsallagh is another in a long line of fine parkland courses to be built in Ireland. Mount Juliet, the K Club, Druid's Glen, the list gets longer every year. Rathsallagh can easily be added to that list. Nor is it inferior amongst the aforementioned layouts.

McEvoy and O'Connor Jnr have created one of the best conditioned courses you will play anywhere. Built to USGA specifications, Rathsallagh is normally always in good shape. It's also one of the more demanding parkland courses you are likely to play.

Measuring close to 7,000 yards, Rathsallagh is not a course the high handicapper should play from the back tees. Anyone brave enough to play the course at its full length had better be a good player, a very good player.

Here you will find man-sized holes, with at least four holes in excess of 450-yards. That this course will be no pushover is obvious from the very first hole, which is a genuine three shot par-5 of 571-yards A lot of players won't be attacking the pin with a mere flick of the wedge. The fact that the second stretches to 454-yards foreshadows the test that lies in store.

However, while the length may have you hitting longer irons than you feel comfortable with, you should have no excuse around the greens, which are among the best you'll find. At Rathsallagh you don't have to hit your putts, a good stroke should send the ball off on a true line to the hole. If you can't putt at Rathsallagh, you can't putt anywhere.

COURSE INFORMATION & FACILITIES

Rathsallagh Golf Club
Dunlavin,
Co. Wicklow.

Director of Golf: Michael Bermingham.
Tel: 045-403316. Fax: 045-403295.

Green Fees:
Weekdays – IR£30. Weekends: IR£40.
Restrictions apply at weekends.

CARD OF THE COURSE – PAR 72

1	2	3	4	5	6	7	8	9	Out
571	454	400	173	396	502	176	382	447	3501
Par 5	Par 4	Par 4	Par 3	Par 4	Par 5	Par 3	Par 4	Par 4	Par 36

10	11	12	13	14	15	16	17	18	In
465	519	390	153	351	382	536	169	450	3415
Par 4	Par 5	Par 4	Par 3	Par 4	Par 4	Par 5	Par 3	Par 4	Par 36

HOW TO GET THERE

Take M50 south from Dublin,
[...] south to M7 south, exit to
[...] south. At end of M9
[...]ntinue on two-lane
[...]hway for 6 miles until
[...]nposts for Rathsallagh
[...]gin.

Rathsallagh House

Rathsallagh House is a four star Grade A Country House set on 530 acres of mature parkland and surrounded by the magnificent Rathsallagh Golf Club. To maintain a happy and relaxed atmosphere, there are only 17 en-suite bedrooms. The House is centrally heated throughout and has large open fires in the dining room, sitting rooms and bar. It has a heated indoor swimming pool, sauna, tennis court, billiard room and fully equipped conference room. Horse riding, clay pigeon shooting, archery and hunting are available by prior arrangement.

Rathsallagh House, Dunlavin, Co. Wicklow
Tel: + 353 (0)45 403112 Fax: + 353 (0)45 403343

Woodbrook

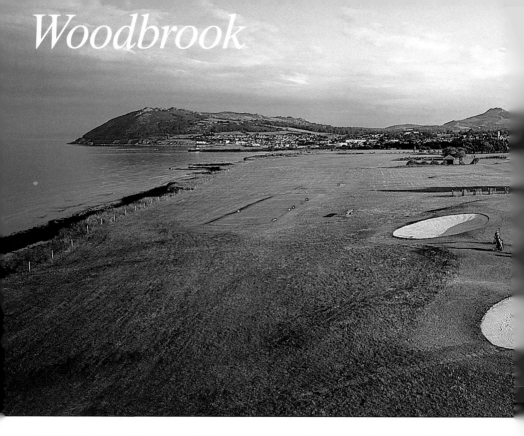

Woodbrook is on one of the most scenic spots near Ireland's capital. Situated at the holiday town of Bray, the Woodbrook course sits on high cliffs that provide fantastic views of Dublin Bay.

The golf course dates back to 1921, when it was just a nine hole course. Another nine were added in 1927, and the course gradually grew in reputation until it was a regular venue for Irish tournaments. For example, the Irish Open has been staged here a number of times, as well as the Irish Professional Championship, not to mention numerous amateur championships.

Although situated beside the sea, Woodbrook is not a links course but a pure parkland layout. Over the years, the club's committee has made a number of changes to toughen up the course. In other words, don't

go there expecting to tear the place apart. Although just short of 6,600 yards, there are a lot of tough holes at Woodbrook.

The best stretch of holes is to be found beside the cliffs after you start the back nine. For example, the 416-yard, par-4, 10th is a hole that should be given as much respect as it deserves. Only two perfect shots will reach the green.

The 15th is another that will require you utmost attention, for a slight lapse in concentration can see your ball on the beach a long way below the fairway.

Although there are some tough holes, Woodbrook does offer the chance of a good score. You will find quite a few par-4s that require just a drive and a medium or short iron. With the exception of the 184-yard, 2nd hole, the par-3s don't require you to hit towering long irons.

HOW TO GET THERE

om the south, take the road
 Shankill as you enter Bray.
om the city, take the first
t for Bray off the N11,
ning left at the
undabout.

COURSE INFORMATION & FACILITIES

Woodbrook Golf Club
Bray,
Co. Wicklow.

Secretary:
Tel: 01-2824799.

Golf Professional Tel: 01-2824799.

Green Fees:
Weekdays – IR£25. Weekends – IR£35.

CARD OF THE COURSE – PAR 72

1	2	3	4	5	6	7	8	9	Out
502	184	375	382	556	382	456	358	140	3335
Par 5	Par 3	Par 4	Par 4	Par 5	Par 4	Par 4	Par 4	Par 3	Par 36
10	11	12	13	14	15	16	17	18	In
416	164	530	209	526	434	486	130	352	3247
Par 4	Par 3	Par 5	Par 3	Par 5	Par 4	Par 5	Par 3	Par 4	Par 36

123

Druids Glen

*T*he Murphy's Irish Open was held at Druids Glen for the first time in 1996. Colin Montgomerie was the winner that year and, not surprisingly, he loved the place. Montgomerie loves courses which put a premium on accuracy, but then he would do – he very rarely misses a fairway.

Course architects Pat Ruddy and Tom Craddock were given a brief to "build the best inland course in Ireland". Whether or not they have is matter of opinion – suffice it to say that Montgomerie probably thinks it is – but it's certainly one of the toughest.

Set on the Woodstock estate some 25 miles from Dublin, Druid's Glen gets its name from a wooded valley said to be an ancient Druid spiritual site. In fact, the par-3, 12th hole is supposedly where the Druid's conducted their pagan ceremonies.

Montgomery won the first Murphy's Irish Open at Druid's Glen with an aggregate score of 279, 5-under par. In days when European Tour events are won with scores in the minus teens, 5-under is quite high. It also tells you something about the course – it's extremely tough. You'll need to have every part of your game on song if you hope to play well at Druid's Glen, especially from the back tees. You'll need to drive it long and straight, play your approach shots well and chip and putt to the best of your ability. Otherwise content yourself with a nice walk around an immaculate course set in pleasant surroundings.

CARD OF THE COURSE – PAR 71

1	2	3	4	5	6	7	8	9	Out
445	190	339	446	517	476	405	166	389	3373
Par 4	Par 3	Par 4	Par 4	Par 5	Par 4	Par 4	Par 3	Par 4	Par 35

10	11	12	13	14	15	16	17	18	In
440	522	174	471	399	456	538	203	450	3653
Par 4	Par 5	Par 3	Par 4	Par 4	Par 4	Par 5	Par 3	Par 4	Par 36

HOW TO GET THERE

n the N11 south from Dublin take the
ay signposted Newtown Mount Kennedy
ewcastle Hospital. Keep following the
n finger signs to Gleann Na Draoite
ch is Druids Glen in Gaelic).
course is situated approx.
inutes from
lin City South.

The European Club

The building of new links courses, bona fide links courses, are rare commodities in recent times. Most of the old traditional seaside courses were built at the turn of the century. Yet Ireland has been blessed with more than its fair share of links courses built in the last 30 or so years. Ballyliffin, Seapoint, Connemara, Murvagh, and The European Club are just a few. Best amongst these is arguably The European Club.

Located about 30 miles south of Dublin in County Wicklow, this outstanding course at Brittas Bay is the creation of Pat Ruddy. Ruddy is a journalist turned golf course architect who has poured his whole life into The European Club. Ruddy had always dreamed of designing a links course, and set out to create a course that would be ranked amongst the best in the world. He is the sole owner of The European Club and although

it was only opened in 1993, his layout is already being mentioned in the same breath as Ballybunion, Portmarnock and Royal County Down.

The European Club is a traditional link course played through glorious sand dunes, with views of the Irish Sea from 17 holes. However, its main difference from the old style links layouts is that you won't find any blind shots on Ruddy's layout. On most holes, what you see is what you get; in other words, everything lies before you. There are a lot of elevated tees that allow you to get a full picture of the hole before you hit your tee shot.

Already the European Club is ranked among the best courses in Ireland - indeed in the British Isles. Ruddy has also designed or co-designed a number of courses in Ireland, but The European may be his best.

COURSE INFORMATION & FACILITIES

The European Club
Brittas Bay,
Co. Wicklow.

Secretary: Sidon Ruddy.
Tel: 0404-47415. Fax: 0404-47449.

Green Fees:
Weekdays – IR£25. Weekends – IR£30.
Weekdays (day) – IR£40. Weekends (day) – IR£45.

CARD OF THE COURSE – PAR 71

1	2	3	4	5	6	7	8	9	Out
390	160	480	430	395	185	435	410	420	3305
Par 4	Par 3	Par 5	Par 4	Par 4	Par 3	Par 4	Par 4	Par 4	Par 35

10	11	12	13	14	15	16	17	18	In
415	385	420	540	165	380	415	390	445	3555
Par 4	Par 4	Par 4	Par 5	Par 3	Par 4	Par 4	Par 4	Par 4	Par 36

HOW TO GET THERE

1 South 30 miles from
ntral Dublin. At Jack White's
, turn left into Brittas Bay.
T junction at Beach, turn
ht & go 1.5 miles to Links.

The Royal Dublin

Royal Dublin was the first club to have an 18 hole course in all of Ireland, when it was laid out in 1885 in Dublin's Phoenix Park. In 1890 it moved to its present site at Bull Island, on links land that was perfect for golf.

The club was moved because Phoenix Park became too boggy in winter. Bull Island had perfect turf for golf. It was the same then as it is today – you won't find better turf than that at Royal Dublin.

In 1914 the course was taken over by the military to help in the war effort. The club was paid compensation by the army after the war and a decision was taken to hire Harry Colt to oversee the redevelopment. Colt is responsible for many great courses around the world, and he did not disappoint at Royal Dublin.

The course has been at the centre of Irish golf since its inception. No fewer than six times has it staged the Irish Open – in 1931, '36, '50, '83, '84 and 1985, the last on the club's centenary. Seve Ballesteros won the tournament that year, the second time in three years he had won the Irish Open at Royal Dublin.

It was fitting that Ballesteros won twice here, because Royal Dublin is home to Ireland's most famous golfer, Christy O'Connor, or "Himself", as he is referred to throughout Ireland. Like Ballesteros, O'Connor is one of the most natural golfers in the world. He perfected his talent at Royal Dublin.

The course is actually quite flat for a links. It looks fairly innocuous at first glance. Be warned, though, for there is danger lurking. What you often miss from the tee are the bunkers, for which Royal Dublin is noted. Avoid them and you will have a chance of playing well.

DUBLIN

CARD OF THE COURSE (metres) – PAR 72									
1	2	3	4	5	6	7	8	9	Out
351	430	360	257	389	170	322	440	160	2779
Par 4	Par 5	Par 4	Par 3	Par 4	Par 3	Par 4	Par 5	Par 3	Par 35
10	11	12	13	14	15	16	17	18	In
374	483	172	381	439	390	241	341	430	3251
Par 4	Par 5	Par 3	Par 4	Par 5	Par 4	Par 4	Par 4	Par 4	Par 37

HOW TO GET THERE

...yal Dublin is on an island 3
...les from the centre of Dublin
...y. It is reached by a wooden
...dge off the main north
...blin Bay road.

oyal Dublin
Golf Club

The K Club

If you're looking for a first class hotel and a first rate golf course near Dublin, then look no further than The K Club.

Arnold Palmer was the man called in to design a golf course on the land that borders the River Liffey and which surrounds Straffan House, now a five star hotel. He has done a good job, too. For while the hotel will cater to your every need, the course should satisfy your golf cravings.

The K Club is a good enough course to have hosted the Smurfit European Open for a number of years. That's really not too surprising – Dr Michael Smurfit owns the course and the hotel.

No expense was spared on The K Club. While they did have problems with drainage early on, these have been overcome. Parkland in nature, the course winds its way through the lovely estate. Not surprisingly, the holes along the River Liffey are the ones that will remain in the memory.

The par-5, 7th and par-4, 8th holes sit by the river on the front nine, and of the two the 7th is perhaps the harder. This hole call for a delicate third shot to be played over the Liffey. Hook at the next and you will be in Ireland's most famous river, for the river runs all the way down the left hand side of this fairway.

On the back nine the Liffey comes into play on the 17th. Here the river threatens any shot hit to the right hand side of the fairway. However, at no more than 395-yards long, the previous hole, the 16th, is perhaps the best on the course. Keep the ball away from the right side of the fairway off the tee and you should keep it dry. Although then you face a shot over water to find the green.

Besides the Liffey, there is a lot more water at The K Club. So take lots of balls.

COURSE INFORMATION & FACILITIES

The K Club
Straffan,
Co. Kildare.

Director of Golf: Paul Crowet.
Tel: 01-6273111. Fax: 01-6273990.

Golf Professional Tel: 01-6273111.

Green Fees:
Weekdays – IR£110. Weekends – IR£110.
Weekdays (day) – IR£110. Weekends (day) – IR£110.

CARD OF THE COURSE – PAR 72

1	2	3	4	5	6	7	8	9	Out
584	408	173	402	213	446	606	375	434	3641
Par 5	Par 4	Par 3	Par 4	Par 3	Par 4	Par 5	Par 4	Par 4	Par 36

10	11	12	13	14	15	16	17	18	In
418	413	170	568	416	447	395	173	518	3518
Par 4	Par 4	Par 3	Par 5	Par 4	Par 4	Par 4	Par 3	Par 5	Par 36

HOW TO GET THERE

...e N4/M4 from Dublin
...ort, exit motorway for
...as. Continue for 5 miles,
...ss Clane Road and follow
...n for Straffan,
...ntinue through
...age and hotel
...n right.

Luttrellstown Castle

*L*uttrellstown Castle is another of those Irish golf courses created on a former country estate with a large mansion house, in this case a castle, on the grounds. Adare Manor, the K-Club, Mount Juliet, are just a few others. The difference between Luttrellstown and those mentioned is that Luttrellstown did not get a big name designer to create the golf course.

You won't find Nicholas Bielenberg's name attached to the design of many golf courses - just one. Bielenberg manages the entire Luttrellstown Estate, and it was he who came up with design for the golf course. He was helped by Edward Connaughton, an expert in golf course agronomy.

The two men have created a layout that is surprisingly good, given their alleged lack of expertise. They've designed a course that

measures just over 7,000 yards to a par of 72, with two equal 36s on the outward and inward nines.

Luttrellstown Castle itself once hosted Queen Victoria and Princess Grace of Monaco, among other notables. Originally built in 1436, the castle has been fully modernised into a fine hotel.

Only laid out in 1994 and opened in 1995, it will be some time before Luttrellstown comes into its own. Many trees have been planted which in time will provide better definition for the fairways and the greens.

Similar to courses like Adare, Mount Juliet and the K-Club, water features heavily on a number of holes at Luttrellstown. So although you feel as if you can open your shoulders a bit, it doesn't pay to be too wayward.

COURSE INFORMATION & FACILITIES

Luttrellstown Castle Golf & Country Club
Castleknock,
Dublin 15.

Director: Graham Campbell.
Tel: 01-808-9988. Fax: 01-808-9989.

Golf Professional
Tel: 01-808-9988. Fax: 01-808-9989.

Green Fees:
Weekdays – IR£35. Weekends – IR£40.
Weekdays (day) – IR£55. Weekends (day) – IR£60.

CARD OF THE COURSE – PAR 72

1	2	3	4	5	6	7	8	9	Out
384	472	386	352	338	202	358	127	508	3127
Par 4	Par 5	Par 4	Par 4	Par 4	Par 3	Par 4	Par 3	Par 5	Par 36

10	11	12	13	14	15	16	17	18	In
171	325	526	403	396	415	153	493	375	3257
Par 3	Par 4	Par 5	Par 4	Par 4	Par 4	Par 3	Par 5	Par 4	Par 36

HOW TO GET THERE

– Dublin City Centre, exit
at M50 (south), exit left
Castleknock – right at
ndabout (Auburn Avenue),
ight on at mini-roundabout,
at lights, left at
OS Pub,
at lights,
ow road.

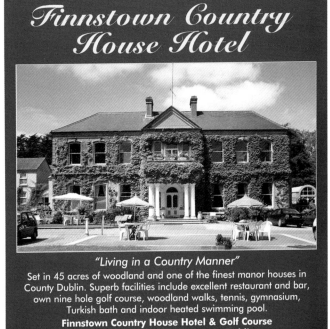

Portmarnock

Portmarnock has hosted more professional tournaments than just about any other in the Emerald Isle. Seven times it has hosted the Irish Professional Championship, 11 times the Irish Amateur, 18 times the Irish Open. It has also been the venue for the Canada Cup, the Walker Cup and countless other events, both amateur and professional.

That Portmarnock has been venue to the top golfers in Ireland and around the world is entirely fitting, for this is one of the most demanding links courses you are ever likely to play. Harold Hilton, who won the Open Championship in 1892 and 1897 and who was one of the greatest amateur players ever, once called the Portmarnock layout "the most natural in the world."

You will agree with Hilton once you play the course, for this is true links golf at its best. It's not surprising that some of the most naturally gifted golfers have won at

Portmarnock – Sam Snead, Arnold Palmer, Ben Crenshaw, Jose Maria Olazabal, Seve Ballesteros and Ian Woosnam are just a few of the professionals to triumph on this magnificent layout. It takes creativity and imagination to tame Portmarnock's links, something the above players have in abundance.

Eighteen great holes are what you will find at Portmarnock, but if one is to be highlighted it has to be the par-3, 15th. This hole measures 187-yards, all of which runs alongside the Irish Sea. Hit the ball right and you could land on the beach; left and you find yourself in a big swale from where par is extremely difficult. Short and you will be playing from tough bunkers. Needless to say it is an elusive green. Rest assured, a three here is a great score.

Portmarnock is on everyone's "must play" list, so make sure you write a letter to the secretary long before you want to play.

CARD OF THE COURSE – PAR 72

1	2	3	4	5	6	7	8	9	Out
355	346	351	403	364	550	168	364	399	3300
Par 4	Par 4	Par 4	Par 4	Par 4	Par 5	Par 3	Par 4	Par 4	Par 36

10	11	12	13	14	15	16	17	18	In
341	392	139	516	350	173	480	429	377	3197
Par 4	Par 4	Par 3	Par 5	Par 4	Par 3	Par 5	Par 4	Par 4	Par 36

HOW TO GET THERE

ublin airport to Malahide.
alahide to Portmarnock.
rtmarnock Golf Club, Golf
ad. (Sign posted).

Portmarnock Links

I t's hard to imagine that you could find two great links courses within literally yards of each other, yet that's what you will find at Portmarnock.

It was always the case that there was more than enough good links land for just the 18 holes that Portmarnock Golf Club occupied. So Mark McCormack's International Management Group acquired some of that good links land and gave Bernhard Langer a crack at creating a first rate seaside golf course. Langer's done just that.

Along with architect Stan Eby, Langer has created a layout to give the older, established Portmarnock Golf Club a run for its money. He has fashioned a par-72, 6,777 yard course that will test the very best.

Like most good new links courses, the new course at Portmarnock looks as if it's been there for a 100 years. Langer has ensured that the course looks as natural as it should given the land it sits on. Great care has been taken to make the course look and feel as traditional as possible. There are no long walks between green and tee and the bunkering is equal to that of the very best seaside layout. Each of the 100 or so bunkers have been carefully revetted, so that you feel as though you're at Muirfield or Carnoustie.

The land the course sits on once belonged to the Jameson family, they of the fine whiskey. Fittingly, James Jameson is buried not far from the first tee and the Jameson family home is now the Portmarnock Country Club Hotel.

COURSE INFORMATION & FACILITIES

Portmarnock Links Golf Club
Portmarnock,
Co. Dublin.

Secretary/Manager: John Quigley.
Tel: 01-846-1800. Fax: 01-846-1077.

Green Fees:
IR £45 per person.

CARD OF THE COURSE (metres) – PAR 71

1	2	3	4	5	6	7	8	9	Out
320	329	178	527	431	486	412	342	156	3181
Par 4	Par 4	Par 3	Par 5	Par 4	Par 5	Par 4	Par 4	Par 3	Par 36

10	11	12	13	14	15	16	17	18	In
484	419	329	137	317	364	371	185	408	3014
Par 5	Par 4	Par 4	Par 3	Par 4	Par 4	Par 4	Par 3	Par 4	Par 35

HOW TO GET THERE

m Dublin Airport turn left
first roundabout, Belfast
ad – take inside lane, exit
ht to Malahide, look out
signs Portmarnock Hotel
Golf Links, 1¹/₂ miles turn
at lights.

North East

The North East

*O*nce you get to Dublin, there really aren't a lot of excuses to go anywhere else. What with the Guinness, the Jameson's, the nightlife and the atmosphere, why would you want to go anywhere else? Golfers are lucky – we have more excuses to venture out of the country's capital than most. For to the north of the city, just a short drive away, are a handful of the best courses you will find anywhere. It's a mixture of the old and the new, and it's a mixture that will appeal to any true golf aficionado. Starting with the old, to the north of the capital lie two true hidden gems, links courses both that will thrill the traditionalist. The first lies in the shape of The Island at Malahide. Here you will find a true links course with all the characteristics you expect to find on a seaside golf course. High dunes, fast running fairways, pot bunkers and slick greens. Oh, and wind, always the wind to contend with. County Louth is another course where the wind plays a factor. This is one of the truest of Ireland's hidden gems. It's a links course that Irish golfers have known about for years, but only in recent times has it attracted visitors from overseas. In other words, phone ahead to book a round for County Louth is getting busier as the word spreads of its charms. By the way, if you hear it referred to as Baltray, don't worry, like many Irish courses it is known by both names. Hard by County Louth lies Seapoint, one of Ireland's many new courses. Designed by veteran European Tour professional Des Smyth, Seapoint is a course that is a mixture of links and parkland golf. Smyth saved the best until last for the closing holes run beside the Irish sea, providing as good a links test as you will find anywhere. St Margaret's and Glasson Golf & Country Club are the other two newer courses to the north of the city that are worth playing. Glasson is the work of Christy O'Connor Jnr, while St Margaret's was designed by Pat Ruddy and Tom Craddock, a twosome responsible for a number of good Irish courses. In other words, they're both worth playing. Best of all, a round at any of theses course - or

*ven two of them – allows you plenty of time to get into Dublin in the evening.
What more could you want?*

ST. MARGARET'S
ISLAND CLUB
COUNTY LOUTH

SEAPOINT
GLASSON

St. Margaret's

Pat Ruddy and Tom Craddock seem intent on making themselves the best golf design partnership in Ireland. They've already impressed with Druid's Glen, where the Irish Open has been held, and they've done an excellent job on St. Margaret's not far from the centre of Dublin.

It's not unusual to find water on many of Ireland's newer courses, but it is unusual to find one hole with three water hazards. That is exactly what you will find on the 525-yard, par-5 8th hole at St. Margaret's. This hole features a lake to the left off the tee, a lake to the right that comes into play on the second shot, and a third lake fronting the green. Needless to say it is one of the most unique holes in Irish golf, one that will remain in your memory long after your visit.

The 8th hole is just one of five par-5s at St. Margaret's. Along with four par-3s and nine par-4s, it makes par for the course 73. As you've probably gleaned from the description of the 8th, water features prominently on this course. Play it from the back tees on an off day and you will lose a lot of balls. Your last might be used on the 18th, where your approach shot has to flirt with a large pond fronted by a lake.

St. Margaret's has been built to the highest of standards, as is expected of any course Ruddy and Craddock put their names to. Conditions are first class, so good that the club hosted the top European women golfers when the Irish Holidays Open was held there in 1994 and 1995. Given the difficulty of the layout, it's not surprising that big hitting Laura Davies took the title both years.

COURSE INFORMATION & FACILITIES

St. Margaret's Golf & Country Club
St. Margaret's,
Co. Dublin.

Reservations Manager: Gillian Harris.
Tel: 01-8640400. Fax: 01-8640289.

Golf Professional Tel: 01-8640400.

Green Fees:
Weekdays – IR£40. Weekends – IR£40.
Weekdays (day) – IR£60. Weekends (day) – IR£60.

CARD OF THE COURSE – PAR 73

1	2	3	4	5	6	7	8	9	Out
358	149	509	456	174	458	374	525	398	3401
Par 4	Par 3	Par 5	Par 4	Par 3	Par 4	Par 4	Par 5	Par 4	Par 36

10	11	12	13	14	15	16	17	18	In
395	366	474	194	402	180	535	512	458	3516
Par 4	Par 4	Par 5	Par 3	Par 4	Par 3	Par 5	Par 5	Par 4	Par 37

HOW TO GET THERE

...iles from Dublin Airport.
...e Belfast Road. Turn left at
...t roundabout, follow road
...4 miles and signs to the
...f course.

GROUP RATES
AVAILABLE ON REQUEST

Please contact
Andrea Molloy/
Pauline Corcoran
on

00 353 1 844 4211

The Island

W hen Philip Walton isn't competing on the European Tour, he resides in the town of Malahide, just north of Dublin. Although he's normally spending precious time with his family, Walton sometimes sneaks off to play The Island Golf Club. Indeed, if you see a strange figure putting on the smooth sands of Malahide Beach, it's probably Walton. The 1995 Ryder Cup hero says the sand provides the perfect surface for grooving a putting stroke.

Mind you, The Island's greens aren't too shabby either.

Historically The Island was always a traditional links course in every sense of the word. Founded in 1890, it was characterised by high sand dunes, fast running links land and numerous blind shots. The club was

happy with the first two elements, but in th[e] late 1980s a decision was taken to do something about the third factor.

It was felt that there were too many blind shots on The Island course to make i[t] compatible with the 20th century. So on th[e] advice of Eddie Hackett and Fred Hawtree revisions were made to reduce the number[s]. You will find no more than about four today, depending of course on where you drive the ball.

The Island is another of those Irish courses that is little known outside Ireland, yet here is a first class links course. Par is 71, and it offers a mix of holes you won't find too often. There are only two par-5s and three par-3s, so if you like your golf to be of the two shot variety, then you'll enjoy The Island's 13 par-4s.

HOW TO GET THERE

...e the main Dublin/Belfast
...d. 3 miles past Swords
...e the road to
...nabate/Portrane, and
...ow signs to the
...nd Golf Club.

COURSE INFORMATION & FACILITIES

The Island Golf Club
Corballis, Donabate,
Co. Dublin.

Secretary/Manager: John Finn.
Tel: 01-8436462. Fax: 01-8436860.

Golf Professional Tel: 01-8436205.

Green Fees:
Weekdays – IR£35. Weekends – IR£45.
Weekdays (day) – IR£45. Weekends (day) – N/A.

CARD OF THE COURSE (metres) – PAR 72

1	2	3	4	5	6	7	8	9	Out
396	363	405	320	336	300	403	282	159	2964
Par 4	Par 4	Par 4	Par 4	Par 4	Par 4	Par 4	Par 4	Par 3	Par 35

10	11	12	13	14	15	16	17	18	In
500	284	379	191	315	507	140	388	410	3114
Par 5	Par 4	Par 4	Par 3	Par 4	Par 5	Par 3	Par 4	Par 4	Par 36

County Louth

ot far from Dublin, just north of the Town of Drogheda, lies a links course that has remained virtually undiscovered by the hordes of golfers who descend on Ireland every year. Yet County Louth at Baltray, which it is often called, is worth the 6,000 or 7,000 mile round trip many golfers make for the pleasure of teeing it up in Ireland.

Irish golfers know how good the course is, as do some foreigners. They know that the course initially laid out in 1890 and later redesigned by Tom Simpson in 1938 is worth the effort it takes to get there. Simpson was responsible for such other great courses as Cruden Bay, Royal Aberdeen and Ballybunion. That's enough to have any serious golfer seeking out County Louth.

It is on this course that the East of Ireland Championship has been held since 1941. This is a 72-hole amateur championship that has been won by some very good players indeed. Joe Carr won the inaugural East of Ireland, and went on to win 11 more times. Current European Tour pros Darren Clarke and Raymond Burns have also won the event.

What the players find when they get to Baltray is a links course with among the best greens in all of Ireland. The contouring of the putting surfaces is such that you'll have done remarkably well if you survive the round without one three-putt.

The par-3s at Baltray are particularly good as each plays in a different direction. The two on the outward call medium iron shots but are played from exposed tees to plateau greens.

Of the par-4s, probably the most memorable is the 14th, a 332-yarder played off a high tee. It's not so much the challenge that makes this hole as the superb views over a long sandy beach and the distant Mourne Mountain near Royal County Down.

miles north east of town of
ogheda.

Co. Louth
Golf Club

COURSE INFORMATION & FACILITIES

Co. Louth Golf Club
Baltray, Drogheda,
Co. Louth.

Secretary/Manager: Michael Delany.
Tel: 041-22329. Fax: 041-22969.

Golf Professional Tel: 041-22444.

Green Fees:
Weekdays – IR£38. Weekends – IR£45.
Weekdays (day) – IR£38. Weekends (day) – IR£45.

CARD OF THE COURSE – PAR 73

1	2	3	4	5	6	7	8	9	Out
433	482	544	344	158	531	163	407	419	3481
Par 4	Par 5	Par 5	Par 4	Par 3	Par 5	Par 3	Par 4	Par 4	Par 37

10	11	12	13	14	15	16	17	18	In
398	481	410	421	332	152	388	179	541	3302
Par 4	Par 5	Par 4	Par 4	Par 4	Par 3	Par 4	Par 3	Par 5	Par 36

Seapoint

*L*ike his great playing competitor Christy O'Connor Jnr, Ireland's Des Smyth has been around golf long enough to know a few things about golf course design. It wasn't surprising then that he soon turned his hand to architecture. The members of Seapoint Golf Club are glad he did.

Smyth hails from nearby Drogheda, so he knew the land the course now occupies. It's land just beyond the beach where Smyth plays with his children when he's not lugging his sticks around the European Tour making a living.

Seapoint is on good links land perfect for golf. Indeed, it sits next door to County Louth, one of Ireland's unsung gems. Seapoint hasn't quite matured to the same standard as Louth – that would be asking a bit much. Nevertheless, it is a fine golf course that will please every level of golfer, from scratch player to high handicapper.

The land at Seapoint is pure, genuine links. However, the opening nine take on the appearance of a fine parkland layout. You won't find many water hazards on true links courses, but there are six on the first nine holes at Seapoint. There are also mature trees on some of the opening holes, further enhancing the feeling that you are playing a parkland course. Don't despair, for there are good links holes here to whet your appetite.

The back nine is more linkslike than the front, with many holes in good duneland. For example, the 180-yard, par-3, 17th hole plays along side the beach, and is one of the best seaside par-3s you'll find anywhere.

Smyth has designed a handful of good courses in Ireland, but Seapoint may be his best.

COURSE INFORMATION & FACILITIES

Seapoint Golf Club
Termonfeckin, Drogheda,
Co. Louth.

Manager: Seamus Kelly.
Tel: 041-22333. Fax: 041-22331.

Golf Professional Tel: 041-22333.

Green Fees:
Weekdays – IR£22.50.
Weekdays (day) – IR£27.50.

CARD OF THE COURSE (metres) – PAR 72

1	2	3	4	5	6	7	8	9	Out
356	494	405	386	182	336	405	466	185	3215
Par 4	Par 5	Par 4	Par 4	Par 3	Par 4	Par 43	Par 5	Par 3	Par 36

10	11	12	13	14	15	16	17	18	In
480	344	407	412	384	146	334	164	453	3124
Par 5	Par 4	Par 4	Par 4	Par 4	Par 3	Par 4	Par 3	Par 5	Par 36

HOW TO GET THERE

>m Dublin, head north on N1 to
>gheda. Continue on N1 over
yne River to traffic lights.
>ceed straight over and after
0yds turn right to Termonfeckin
>nce there go over hump back
▪dge and turn
▪ht for club.

Situated in the heart of the historical town of Drogheda – a town centre hotel of character and distinction

A old fashioned warm welcome awaits you at The Westcourt Hotel, and luxury abounds throughout – all guest accommodation is furnished to the highest standard with prices that will keep you happy and ample private car parking available.

All bedrooms provide:

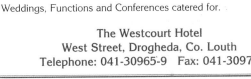

- En-suite facilities
- Remote control TV with satellite channels
- Direct dial telephone
- Tea/coffee making facilities

A choice of restaurants and entertainment are on offer with something to suit all tastes.

Weddings, Functions and Conferences catered for.

The Westcourt Hotel
West Street, Drogheda, Co. Louth
Telephone: 041-30965-9   Fax: 041-30970

Glasson

While Irish golf and great scenery almost go hand in hand, don't think that golf courses with great views are only restricted to the seaside. There's beauty to be found inland as well.

Glasson Golf and Country Club is just one of many excellent Irish courses where the scenery is quite simply spectacular.

Christy O'Connor Jnr is responsible for the Glasson layout, and he was blessed with 175 acres of land that provides some of the best views in all of Ireland. Glasson is situated beside Killinure Bay on Lough Ree, a large inland lake some 17 miles long which is connected to the River Shannon.

O'Connor Jnr has made good use of the land he was given to produce a par-72 course that measures just over 7,000 yards. (So good that the bay or the lough is visible from all 18 holes.) Here you will find a good variety of golf, including a good mix of long and short holes. The third is perhaps one of the best so called short holes. This a 219-yard, par-3 that has to be played over a swale to a plateau green with Lough Ree providing a superb backdrop. After two fairly generous opening holes, you know the game is on at the third. Glasson just gets better as you proceed to the 19th hole.

Christy saved his best efforts for the last half dozen holes, holes which provide magnificent views of the lough, especially from the back tee at the par-5, 14th. Here the tee is situated on high ground, from where you are provided with a panoramic view of Killinure Bay. The bay even comes into play for the approach shot, as it lies near the left side of the green.

Don't worry about the golf – the walk will be just fine.

COURSE INFORMATION & FACILITIES

Glasson Golf & Country Club
Glasson, Athlone,
Co. Westmeath.

Operations Manager: Fidelma Reid.
Tel: 0902-85120. Fax: 0902-85444.

Green Fees:
Weekdays – IR£24. Weekends – IR£27.

CARD OF THE COURSE – PAR 72

1	2	3	4	5	6	7	8	9	Out
396	552	219	406	199	559	410	432	412	3585
Par 4	Par 5	Par 3	Par 4	Par 3	Par 5	Par 4	Par 4	Par 4	Par 36

10	11	12	13	14	15	16	17	18	In
513	183	406	397	566	185	452	450	383	3535
Par 5	Par 3	Par 4	Par 4	Par 5	Par 3	Par 4	Par 4	Par 4	Par 36

HOW TO GET THERE

₂ hours from Dublin/
lway/Shannon.
niles north of Athlone on
5. Turn left at Glasson
lage Restaurant
d Golf Club is
₂ miles away.

lasson Golf
Country Club

Shamrock Lodge

COUNTRYHOUSE HOTEL

Here in the Shamrock Lodge you are assured of a warm and friendly welcome. The hotel is located just 5 minutes walk from the centre of Athlone Town and is ideally situated between Glasson Golf and Country Club on the east side of Lough Ree and Athlone Golf Club on the west with Mount Temple Golf Club just 5 miles away.

The Shamrock Lodge hotel has 27 bedrooms, all en suite with direct dial telephone, multichannel television, tea and coffee making facilities. The hotel is surrounded by some beautiful gardens with ample car parking facilities for all our guests.

Our Carvery is open daily serving luncheon from 12.30pm to 3.00pm while our Au Luain Restaurant is open nightly from 6.30pm to 9.30pm.

Live music is provided every weekend in our warm and comfortable lounge for our guest's entertainment.

CLONOWN ROAD, ATHLONE, CO. WESTMEATH
Tel: (0902) 94966/92601   Fax: (0902) 92737

THE
Cliff House
HOTEL

A SISTER HOTEL OF THE LISTOWEL ARMS,
NINE MILES FROM LISTOWEL,
IT IS A NATURAL BASE FROM WHICH TO
EXPLORE IRELAND'S SOUTHWEST COAST.

To the north are the Shannon Estuary, the Burren of Clare, the mighty Cliffs of Moher. To the south are the Dingle Peninsula, the Ring of Kerry, the Lakes of Killarney.

Commanding a glorious vantage above Ballybunion Beach, this 'three star' hotel is a golfers home from home with the world ranked Ballybunion Links nearby.

Its Carraig Restaurant offers a wholesome menu of fresh local food, the speciality being seafood served on the day it is caught.

The Cliff House Hotel

BALLYBUNION, COUNTY KERRY
TELEPHONE: 353 (0) 68 27777
FAX: 353 (0) 68 27783

— *O'Callaghan Family Hotels* —
A member of Holiday Ireland Hotels

THE DOWNHILL HOTEL

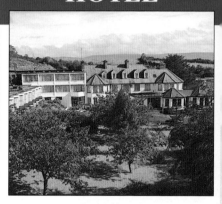

Set in its own magnificent landscaped gardens — a haven of tranquility. This 3 star hotel offers excellent cuisine, personal and friendly service and superb facilities. Accommodation is luxurious with television/video, hairdryer, trouser press, direct dial telephone and tea or coffee making facilities. The Downhill is situated in the heart of a golfer's and fisherman's paradise and is convenient to both Knock and Sligo Airports which are only 35 miles from the hotel. Few could ask for a more enjoyable, challenging or better place to stay. If you are unable to escape from work, the Downhill Hotel offers an excellent opportunity to go from conference to relaxation. The newly renovated "Eagles" Health and Leisure Club with its two swimming pools, steam room, sauna, jacuzzi, sunbed, fully equipped gym, 3 all weather floodlit tennis courts, squash court, table tennis, full size snooker table, aerobic studio, free weights area and children's playroom. For those in search of a more peaceful break pay a visit to the Ceide Fields and experience the oldest farmland in the world dating back to 3000BC — see the famous Foxford Woollen Mills, North Mayo Heritage Centre, Knock Shrine or take a quiet walk on one of the many beautiful sandy beaches. Relax in "Frogs" Piano Bar where international entertainment can be enjoyed Tuesday-Sunday inclusive.

For more information on accommodating your group at the Downhill Hotel please contact Kay Devine on Tel: 00 353 96 21033 or Fax: 00 353 96 21338. Ballina, County Mayo, Ireland

Index

Notes

Notes